DAVID V

CW01507198

SAUCE

First published by Martian Red 2025

First edition

ISBN: 978-1-0369-0263-6

For Dad

Foreword

Hello Dear Reader! Welcome to Sauce! A collection of poems intended to keep you entertained whether you are in bed, bath, or custody or maybe on trains, holiday or drugs.

Although this assemblage covers a range of subjects, you may or may not be glad to know that there are no poems about philosophy, astronomy, political history, gardening, taxidermy, collecting navel fluff or competitive duck herding.

There *are* poems about celebrities, video games, chavs, snobbery, food and breaking wind. Some of these subjects are, though, my fields of expertise!

In several poems, I vary the number of lines in the verses, so they consist of couplets, tercets, quatrains etc in the same poem. Also, the rhyme scheme can change so, for example, the second and fourth lines of a verse can rhyme and in the next verse, it might be that the first pair rhyme and then the second pair... where have you gone? Come back!

Apologies to everybody slighted in this book, including, but not limited to, the following:

Train drivers, posh people, bargain hunters, drug dealers, the overweight, the homeless, snowmen, personal trainers, video gamers, handymen, doctors, toy woodpeckers, mosquitos and James Corden.

This book was written sporadically over a period of three years in seven countries and over fifty towns and cities. And, of course, a thousand cafes and nearly as many cheese toasties!

Thank you for buying, borrowing or stealing this book and I sincerely hope you enjoy it whatever the method of possession. If you've had it as a Christmas present, please don't curse Santa Claus (as I have in this book) as you'll make him angry, and he might give you another copy as a punishment!

A big thank you to everyone for their help and encouragement, to all at Hopes and Beams especially Ian Chalmers, Poetry Whitchurch, The Top Hatters, Creative Crewe, Itch, Cover2Cover, ABDA, Monopoli's, The Curious Cat Bookshop, The Nantwich Bookshop, Jonathan White, Samantha Sanderson-Marshall, Peter Robinson and to Sharon for her support and patience. Also, to the audience members and fellow poets that haven't booed me off the stage (yet)!

Enjoy!

Dave

Credits:

Illustrations: Samantha Sanderson-Marshall
Design: David Vernon/Samantha Sanderson-
Marshall
Photography: Peter Robinson
Published By: Martian Red
Printed By: IngramSpark and Amazon KDP

Contents

Greggsit..13

M.I.A. 17

Fly on the Wall 19

The Yellow Sticker Girl 23

Farting At Dinner 27

Royalty 29

Dirty Washing 31

Dodgers 35

No More Trees 37

Seven Dicks 41

Wear Me Clothes Out 45

Elephant 49

I'll Put The Kettle On! 51

Chav...55

Loose Women...57

Out of Practice 61

Bovril, The Divine 67

L...69

Pack, Man! 71

The Best Pest Controller...75

Spearmint Wino 79

Whale Watching 81

Mange Toucan...89

Binfluencer 91

Dating An Anorexic 95

Rocket Man 101

Stuffed 103

The Overdressed...107

Wind Power...109
Almost Famous 113
Roger The Bodger 117
Yaffle 121
Fifty Shades of Graham 123
Deluded...127
Middle Class Blues 129
Calmer and Karma 133
Do Ya Wanna Buy My Car?...135
The Seagull 139
The Ghosts in the Machines...143
The Loping Opener 145
Go Large 149
2 x 2..151
Village Idiots...159
Fascist Dick Taylor 161
A.M...165
A Day at the Races 167
U Bend, The Rules 171
Snowman and Wife 173
Personal Trainer..177
Chickenshit...181
The Death of a Traffic Warden 185
She's Not Great 191
The Third Person 193
Zen and the Art of Skilful Avoidance...............................195
Posh...199
Miss Treat 203
Santa Banter 205
Lightning Rod 209
I Wanna Be A Train Driver..211

Monster Mensch..213
Which Doctor? 217
Meat and Potato Pilot.......................................221
Me and the Bearded Ladies............................223
Clothes Don't Suit...225
The Kit Kat Man 227
People Are Like Fruit..229
Civil Phwoah..231
It's Time..233
Praise for Sauce 235

Greggsit

My life will never quite be the same
I've fallen out with a bakery chain!
I went into Greggs for a bit of scoff
A little nosebag to take the wind off
The guys on the counter looked at me with a grin
Cos my stomach arrived two minutes before I did!

I said 'One sausage roll please, mate!'
One smirked, 'Don't you want a pack of eight?'
The other said, 'We didn't think you'd want just one!'
Huh! Maybe they thought I'd order a tonne!

Is it cos I'm a bit cuddly, a chubby bunny?
Or did they just want me to spend more money?
Did they think my mouth was a giant black hole?
Sucking everything into it completely whole?

I said 'Empty the ovens! Give me all you've got!'
'I've got a van outside, I'll take the lot!'
'I'll buy and eat all your frigging stock!'
The cheeky sods!

I wish I hadn't been quite so candid!
Cos I stormed out, empty-handed!
The problem is, I'm quite addicted
And now, more than a bit conflicted

But all their contempt and derision
Has helped me come to a decision...

I'm never going in there ever again!
I'm gonna leave, not remain!
I'm doing a Greggsit!
This is my pastry exit!

No queuing with the proles
For scrummy hot sausage rolls
I'm not going to shed a single tear!
I'm not going there for at least a year!

No more thinking 'yum yum!'
When I see a... yum yum
Got other places to buy my lunch!
I'm not going there for at least a month!

It may be beneficial to my health
To resist the bean and sausage melts
A world without pasties may seem bleak
But I'm not going there for at least a week!

Though my resolve will be tested
And my tastebuds bored and rested
I will abstain from all steak bakes!
I'm definitely not going in there today!

No glistening doughnuts or hot bacon baps
I'm strong! There's no way I'm going to relapse...
Oh, sod this!

I'm going over there to give them what for!
I'll just shout at the staff through the door!
Staying away though has been good I reckon
But I suppose I could nip in - for just a second
To ask them why they were mean and callous
To be safe, I'll just stand near the salads...

Oh god, it's no use!
What am I trying to prove?!

Because a few hours without this stuff
My lips go dry and my eyes puff up!
Then there's the itching which drives me up the wall!
All the classic symptoms of pastry withdrawal!

Greggs is paradise, Nirvana, heaven
But thank God mine's not open 24/7!
So there's only one way to get off this stuff...
I'll have to go and get my mouth sewn up!

(I'm off to the new Gregg's theme park now!
I'm going on a sausage rollacoaster!)

M.I.A.

I was on a promise
With a girl called Doris
Arranged to meet in Clacton
But I was missing in Acton!

Clacton's by the sea of course
But I'm not that arsed at all
Cos she said she'd swallow my balls
At 3pm, behind the bingo hall
In Clacton

Twenty-eight fucking degrees
Sick of this fucking heat
Missed my train and connection
Me, the King of Missed Direction
Stuck with a massive erection
In Acton

Fuck my life - always shat on!
No *Kiss-Me-Quick* hat on!
My hands I was sat on!
Stuck. In Acton

Rang Doris but she'd had enough!
When I said I'd missed my train and bus

Angry, hot, at the end of her tether
She was splitting hairs and spitting feathers
Said she was going to blow Eddie Clough
Inside the old, derelict lifeguard's hut
In Clacton

I couldn't get a-fucking-way!
I had to stay all fucking day!
Nada, nowt, nothing doing!
No greasy chips and sweaty screwing!
Inaction
In Acton

No beaches here or penny arcades
Shady people but there is no shade
In Acton
Where are the slags called Doris?
In Clacton!

I just want some satisfaction!
I can't get no satisfaction!
No, I can't get no satisfaction!
Or action
In Acton

Fly on the Wall

Buzzzzzz!
I am the Fly on the Wall!
This fly, with compound eyes, sees all!
I spy on you behind closed doors
I am the Neighbourhood Watch in insect form!

There are twenty houses in this street
Occupied by perverts, weirdos, deadbeats
An assortment of illegal immigrants, thieves and freaks
And this is the *posh* part of town I believe!

No curtain twitching needed; *I'll* give you the goss!
I fly through an open window or letter box
No need for security cameras with *me* around!
I report back on what's going down
Or who is...

Steve lives on the corner and works in a garage
While his wife stays home in a loveless marriage
She waits for visits from her postman there
Who delivers his package to her upstairs!

At No. 6, Mike works nights, Katherine works days
And while the Kat's away, the Mike will play

Has a visiting dominatrix from two til four
Tells his wife *cycling* is what made him saddle
sore!

Kev, over the road, is a dodgy fella
He grows tons of weed in his cellar!
Then sells joints through his kitchen window
He deals more than a croupier in a casino!

Gary, in the bungalow, works six days a week
But he's receiving dole, he's a benefit cheat!
Milks the DWP for all he can get
And has three Somali slaves locked in his shed!

I am the Fly on the Wall!
I see... all!

At No. 3, Sandra chews pills like they're Smarties
And has weekly *Bondage and Tupperware*
parties!
Her bi boyfriend, Phil, invites *Hairy Bears* too
Cos, like me, he often munches on fruits!

Up the road, Bob likes *fencing*, but guess which
sort?
He's never said 'En guard!' or held a flimsy sword!
Never seen him with concrete posts or any panels
of wood!

But he *does* live in an Alladin's Cave, full of stolen goods!
Mr Abbot's gardeners are taking the piss!
All over his garden and in his bins!
Before shooting up or rolling skins
And they sell fake passports for twenty quid!

On the far corner, Glenda lives alone
Barely sees a soul, stays all day at home
Spends most of her time upstairs, under her sheets!
Something in her bedside drawer buzzes, and it isn't me!

Susan, who lives at number thirty-three
Sucks on more than just boiled sweets!
And her garden is kept immaculate with pride
And under the patio, her missing husband lies!

I am the Fly on the Wall!
I see... all!

I've seen it all, I've seen the lot!
But I'm a fluttering, Peeping Tom?!
You say I'm a nosey troublemaker?!
And an irritating, buzzy muckraker?!
You want to swat me?! Ha! I'm too fast!
I will crap on your fruit, lay maggots in your flasks!

And remember I know a few things about *you!*
I could spill the beans on what *you* get up to!
So, look after me and I'll keep schtum
Give me an apple or maybe a plum
Let me land on your peaches and pears
And I'll forget who climbs *your* stairs!
Then maybe I'll stay tight lipped
Because loose lips sink ships
And marriages...
You scratch my back, I'll scratch yours!
Cos I am the Fly on the Wall!
I see all!

The Yellow Sticker Girl

We supermarket shoppers are watchful, primed
It's not long now until closing time!
Slowly shuffling, pretending not to care
Though underneath, we're alert and aware!
Cos when stock is slightly past its best
and it's just about still fresh...

Here she comes! Here she comes!
She's got a loaded pricing gun!
She's come to rock our world!
She's the Yellow Sticker Girl!

The cost of living's up and food's so dear
So we're on our heels when she appears!
We're Usain Bolt down past the veg
To locate her, knocking down the bread!

With such efficiency and grace
She click-clacks and pastes
And then she's pacing, even racing
But we're chasing, craving savings!

She turns a corner and disappears
'Just a minute ago, she was here!'
We ask her colleagues where she went
We're eager beagles, sniffing her scent!

And listening for her stomping steps
A Jewish guy asks, 'Where'd she schlep?'

We punters are roaming and homing in
On her position with military precision!

We're Speedy Gonzales when she breaks cover
And run to her like she's a long-lost lover!
We follow her around, walking a mile
Cos she's the Pied Piper of the aisles!

We grab those bargains and fill our baskets
And hang on the tail of *Lady Fantastic*
In her spell that we're now under
Where will she strike next, we wonder?
Try and predict where she'll stop
But she's just like a spinning top!
Suddenly changing speed and direction
A whirling dervish in the chiller section!

She puts stickers on yogurts, but they are claimed
By the bio-culture vultures straight away
For the cut-price quiche, there are plenty of takers
She's gone again! But she can't shake us!

Whatever happens, we won't lose her!
We're shadowing this *reducer seducer!*
We are her followers, she's our leader!
Us giveaway hunters and discount seekers

And all the usual suspects are here today
Chris The Redeemer and Mean Old Fay
Jason and his Bargainauts and Miserly Sid
Slavering at the prospect of saving a few quid!

I plod nonchalantly, hands behind my back
Pretending not to notice where she's at
Cos aspiring, sophisticated, middle-class are we
Don't want to advertise that we're buying cheap!
We are now, slyly, hiding behind the beans
Waiting for tickets from the little machine
Getting more knock-downs than a boxer!
We are all one deal craving monster!

For we're determined, hell bent!
We are loitering with intent!
Concealed quietly behind the chillers
We're all actors now in this thriller!
Who will get to the bargains first?
All of us Meercats, on our toes, alert!

The supermarket's her theatre and she's on stage
We watch her in awe in her one-woman play
Where the lead sticks on bits of yellow paper
Starring in *Miss Hughes and her Cut-Price
Capers*

Rumours are, that bree will come down again!
A reduction of nearly thirty-five percent!

Buy now or wait for cheaper? Deal or no deal?
With my thirty-pee baguette, it's a total steal!

Suddenly she's left through a side door
Would these bargains be no more?!
But two minutes later, she reappears!
We let out of collective, silent cheer!

Because...

Here she comes! Here she comes!
She's got a loaded pricing gun!
She's come to rock our world!
She's the Yellow Sticker Girl!

Farting At Dinner

There's a code of behaviour you should adopt
When you think you might have *one to drop!*
A useful etiquette for social dining events
To ensure you close your body's own vent!

So, when you're attending a dinner party
Once you're seated, refrain from farting!
If you can prevent it, and are physically able
You should not blow off at the dining table!

You see, it's just not the done thing
To eat while letting your ring sing!
And don't tell your fellow guests, it's not good form
That you've got more wind than a storm!

If you contain more gas than a Russian pipeline
Don't expel your bottom breath when you dine!
If you normally find it hard not to let rip
Before you arrive, hammer a cork in it!

And resist the urge to proudly pump it
Refrain from blowing your own anal trumpet!
You see, it really puts people off their food
If they think you've just followed through!

Someone could choke on their dessert
If you let out a pungent botty burp!
Don't make the other diners suffer
By being a flatulent, toxic, eggy guffer!

You'll want to make a good impression
So don't let them hear your woodwind section!
Nobody wants to feel your wind through their
hair!
Don't cause your host to reupholster their chairs!

So, just to recap
If you are 'with gas'
Don't let your sphincter blast!
Don't raise a cheek, raise a glass!
But if you really can't let the urge pass
Let it out, relax...
And just blame the bloody cat!

Royalty

I can't say that I'm into royalty
It's not really induced a fervour
Never been keen on who is queen
And the only king I care about is Burger!

Dirty Washing

Do launderettes have an erotic charge?
Well, here's my spin on it!

Ladies, do you get wet when you visit the
launderette?
Do you think it's the rumble of the tumble dryer?
Men, does the steam, like an erotic incense, give
you trouser tents?
Does it make everyone orgasm like oyezing Town
Cryers?
So, are we laundretters all moist and rigid?
Or do these places leave us flaccid and frigid?

Today, I'm reporting from the field
To see if it's true or just cobblers!
If it's a myth, I can wash my smalls
If not, I can film a few doggers!

I enter the launderette to nods and stares
And plonk myself down on a plastic chair
I slowly open my laundry bag
A Pandora's box of filthy rags!
Rummaging inside and sifting through it
It emits a whiff of bodily fluids!

Voyeuring each other as we load our clothes
Washing dirty linen in public, feeling exposed
My fellow washers watch me, half-entertained
As I examine my boxers that are covered in stains
I sniff my socks, gag, and then throw them in
Along with a pair of shorts I really should bin!
Ramming the remaining clothes into the machine
Doubting very much that they'll ever come clean
Then pour in the powder which looks like cocaine
Insert the coins; five quid down the drain!
We silently contemplate the hum and the drone
Cursing our broken or lack of washer back home

I'm sat near Scary Mary and Weird Michael
Who both stare at me through the whole cycle
Stood gawping at the laundrette attendant's thighs
Is Wild Billy; lank hair and two glass eyes!

Gail wonders if the dye on her new clothes is fast
And if her brand new relationship with Kevin will
last
The others stare into space or read crappy novels
Glad of the escape from their bedsits and hovels

My eyes fix on the whirl of my jeans
As I zone out in my own daydream
The washer sobs and the clothes swim
The socks dry and the shirts spin

Maybe I should have washed the clothes I have on!
But I'm not going to strip off in front of everyone!
I am certainly not going to do a *Nick Kamen!*
They'd run a mile, and I wouldn't blame 'em!
One girl opens out her sheets for all to see
Revealing a sort of revolting tapestry!
The visible stains are scores from the night before
When her boyfriend gave her one...two, three and four!
She'd spiked his Horlicks with Viagra and Spanish Fly
Highlights of last night's action, replay in her mind!

I notice furtive glances have become stolen!
Are we all becoming damper and swollen?
Cos looks are now provocative and enticing
There's heavy breathing among the excited!

The women's heart rates increase with speed!
And the men have less room in their jeans!
The atmosphere is quickly changing!
Sultry looks and winks exchanging!
A feeling of the consensual and the sensual!
Something fundamental, primal, elemental!

Now my olfactory senses are heightened!
Way above the visual and the textural!

I am turned on by the smell of washing powder!
Daz, Aerial. I'm now an *Omosexual!*

I become a fanatic for the laundry basket!
And a whore for the Lenor!
I don't need a fabric stiffener!
I'm getting a thrill from the conditioner!

This pot's been boiling, now the lid's come off!
Everybody rises and quickly gets their kit off!
I resist, ducking behind a chair to video it all
It's now a fleshy melange of breasts and balls!

They are now actors in this erotic play
Where discarded clothes now cover the stage
Entering not *stage left* but at *every* angle!
Private parts rise, flap and dangle!
At it on benches, chairs, on the machines!
I can't see to film because of the steam!
This is not the place to think about missing socks!
This place is where people go to get their rocks off!

My dryer needs another ten minutes
I contemplate putting another coin in!
But the erotic spectacle unfolds like the sheets
My resistance crumbles. I'm gonna join in!

Sorry about this poem, I should have kept it
clean!!

Dodgers

L.A.

Tax

Fare

Draft

Soap

Fanny

Salad

Jammy

No More Trees

Have you ever wondered how it would be?
If we lived in a world without any trees?

You say 'Dave, we'd not given it any thought!'
'But we're really not that bothered at all!'
Maybe I can convince you to care?!
Lend me your ears, if you've a minute to spare...

Would our riversides, fields and parks look the same?
Would the countryside look a little more plain?

No sounds of the breeze in the leaves of the trees
Less carbon dioxide absorbed, and oxygen released

And could we reduce our carbon footprint angst?
If there were no trees that we could plant?

Where would we doze and picnic in the shade?
And where would lovers carve their names?

These perennial plants would be sorely missed
And the word 'arboretum' would not exist!

Fires would have to burn without logs
What would lumberjacks do for a job?

Where would birds nest and keep their eggs?
Would tree surgeons have to treat *us* instead?

There'd be no fun way to hang our kitchen mugs
Would only swimmers and elephants have trunks?

Our modern lives would be much less richer
They'd be no more timber... just Tinder!

Up what would bored children climb?
And where would flashers lurk behind?

Duncan Goodhew wouldn't have fallen, losing his hair!
And where would the toilets be for all of the bears?

In the park, where would dogs have a slash?
And on what would we grow all our cash?

Notts County fans would call it a dream!
Cos Nottingham would only have *one* football team!

And where would Robin Hood hide?
What would Mr and Mrs Gump have called their child?

They'd be nothing for hippies to hug!
And no surname for Victoria Wood!

There would be no things like linoleum or cork
And what would Keanu Reeve's acting be called?

Nowhere real on which to hang the Christmas decs
Nothing rough against which to have outdoor sex!

Those rainforest destroyers laugh and cock a snook!
Not caring we'd have no papers, magazines or books!
And you say you *still* don't give a fuck?!
Listen!! There'd be no toilet rolls!! *That* woke you up!!

Seven Dicks

I found a genie when I was eight
He said he'd grant me a wish
I considered asking for a new bike
But instead, I said 'I'd like seven dicks!'

So, the very next day when I awoke
I realised that I was now blessed
But the first time I went for a pee
I didn't half make a right mess!

Urination was a sprinkler system
So there was piss all over the walls!
I splashed the windows and the ceiling too
And you should have seen the state of the floor!

And all through school
In the changing rooms
The teasing never stopped!
But I had doubts
That they could count
Cos they called me Octopus Cock!

A few years later, at university
All the girls had become aware
With a reputation in college, it was common
knowledge
That I was packing a lot downstairs!

Then I worked in an office and the ladies said
'You're a seven-seater bike we love to mount!'
We rode together, me and many of those girls
I did HR and half of Accounts!

But they often groped me against my will!
By the copier or when making a brew
And I didn't report them at all, I'm afraid
I am #MeSeven not #MeTwo!

I decided to distract from the way I was packed
And smarten up and be very well dressed
When I got clothes fitted by my tailor, I'd say
'I dress to the right, the middle, and the left!'

With time at least, I could tame my beasts
Cos I've trained them all to behave!
Now, when I'm aroused, I can lie down
And spin seven quite large china plates!

And now I sign autographs and open shops
And everyone in the country knows me!
People come up to me in pubs or the street
And most of them offer to blow me!

As I've got all Seven Wonders of the World
I've always been chased by lots of girls
Those ladies are sporty, if you know what I mean!
And I can simultaneously do a whole netball team!

Shagging multiple girls at once is fantastic!
Though it costs me a fortune in prophylactics
But in unison, I can entertain a bunch of c*nts
And can service the seven dwarves all at once!
(I'd cheer up Grumpy at least!)

You think that it's all great, this circumstance?
No, it's like having a nest of vipers in my pants!
And my boxer shorts have to be custom made!
Seven flies and extra frontal space for my snakes!

I know a guy who had *five* dicks of his own
He was the manager of the band *Boyzone*
So, I'd tell Enid Blyton if she was alive
That *my* Secret Seven is better than *his* Famous
Five!

I've got seven rides for seven lovers
Or seven brides or seven brothers
Just joking lads, I'm not a bummer!
Though I've a knob for each rainbow colour!

There's no limit to my penile reach
Got a schlong for every day of the week!
Some people ask me how it feels
Having your underwear full of eels?

Well, I'm content, I'm a happy camper
Cos my lunch box is more like a hamper!

Do I attract all the ladies? Well, naturally!
Cos I've got more shafts than a darts factory!
Every girl in Scotland wants a taste of ma
porridge!
And I've got more wood than Sherwood Forest!
My magnificent seven will send you to heaven
Cos my dick amplifier goes up to eleven!

So, in recognition of all I've got
I've changed my name to Ivor Multicock!
Cos I've got a one-stop knob shop!
I've always got some tools in stock!

So even though life is so great now
And I really have a sense of purpose
But if I ever get bored, I'm always *packed*
And ready to join the circus!

Wear Me Clothes Out

I think I should be able to wear what I like!
Not just conform to a dumb stereotype!
Donning what society expects me to wear!
I want to put on clothes that make people stare!
And I don't care about fashion faux pas!
Cos I want to walk round looking like an arse!

Llama print Pyjamas under garish silk robes!
Or I'll borrow some of Eddie Izzard's clothes!
Because you can forget about gender norms!
I want a grass skirt made from my front lawn!

Some say 'Get rid of your linen and you're
winning!'
I wanna look crumpled so it's the iron I'll be
binning!
I'll be an unshaven mess and will dress in the
dark!
Or maybe spend nights sleeping rough in the
park!
I can then go for the Geldof or the Corbyn look!
A Worzel Gummidge tribute act, giving zero fucks!

I want to dress down and kill formality
For me, 'mad-casual' will be the normality!
Nothing round my neck, getting ever tighter
Like a *Star Wars* spaceship - I'm a tie fighter!

Because I prefer less restrictive clothing
I want to be relaxed, wherever I'm going
'There's goes a chilled fashionista!' is what they'll
say!
I won't wear a tux, a Chris Moyles or any other
'DJ'!
I want to be vertical and horizontal at the same
time!
So no to Tiger Woods or any other 'black tie'
Geddit? Black Thai? *Suit* yourself...

Maybe I could sport a gold lame shirt
Matched with a zigzag, rah-rah skirt!
But, of course now, pretty much anything goes!
A belt for me trousers with lengths of garden hose!
Wear a gaudy football shirt, maybe like Crystal
Palace!
Or a cropped belly top with a cartoon of a phallus!

A blouse with holes around the nips!
A Rolling Stones t-shirt *without* the lips!
Latex, Playtex
Or see-through keks
Jackboots, a spotty suit
Or even a pair of clown shoes!

I'll try turquoise braces and a dunce's hat
With the most hideous looking cravat!

Or a bikini made entirely of beads
Under tie dye patchwork dungarees!

A suit with a dayglo, leopard print
Clothes to make even Jonathan Ross wince!
Something bright enough to burn out your eyes!
Or that Noel Fielding would think about twice!

Maybe I should consider a gimp mask?
Or a codpiece made from a thermos flask?
I'll wear a wig made from all my old pubes!
Or a rubber scarf made from inner tubes
Recycle an outfit from a green wheelie bin
Or perhaps a jacket made from human skin!

Yes, I'll undoubtedly, look at bit of a ponce!
But I'll be retro and futuristic all at once!
I'll make people smile, give their eyes a treat!
Even if some *will* shout at me in the street!

Cos I'll wear plastics, textiles, metal and wood!
And daub my t-shirts with faeces and blood!
I'll raid charity shops, jumble sales and bric-a-
brac stalls!
Make clothes out of chain mail and cut-up beach
balls!

I'll be prominent and conspicuous!
And look a little bit ridiculous!
But I'll be a one-off, unique!
A singularity, walking down the street!

I'll always look arty and a little bit tarty!
A walking, bad-taste, fancy dress party!

You're worried about my mental state? Surely
not?
You think I may have completely lost the plot?
Well! Just in case you're right, and all my reason
has gone!
Today, I think I'll just shove me jeans and t-shirt
on!

Elephant

Nelly, I sent you to the supermarket but
I can't believe how much you forgot!
And you call yourself an elephant?
You've the memory of a ZX-81!

You said you don't need to write things down!
And you don't need take a list!
But you came back with sweet bugger all!
I'd whack you if you weren't so big!

Did you bring back bread, milk or butter?
No, you just stole some sticky buns!
You had a good feed, then fell asleep
Before showering six shoppers with dung!

And then before you left Sainsbury's
You went *tonto*, absolutely crackers!
Trumpeting and running down the aisles
Trampling three trainee shelf stackers!

But I won't ask you to leave
And go and pack up your trunk!
As long as you do a couple of deeds
To make up for what you've done!

The store said they'd forgive and forget
So you needn't be too saddened!
Provided you sit on Coleen Nolan's head
Cos everyone wants to see her flattened!

So calm your flappy ears my friend!
You'll be staying and not going!
And one more thing! Use your trunk
To strangle Laurence Llewelyn-Bowen!

I'll Put The Kettle On!

Hi, how've you been? Not good, you say?
You've so many problems, you dunno where to
start?
I've got some time, tell me what's on your mind!
Come into the kitchen, you look a little parched!

You've got no power at home? The fuses all blew?
I'll put the kettle on!
Your elderly neighbours are sunbathing in the
nude?
I'll put the kettle on!

You've got the personality of Kier Starmer?
I'll put the kettle on!
You've found out Darth Vader is your father?
I'll put the kettle on!

Your jackpot-winning lottery ticket turned up, a
day too late?
I'll put the kettle on!
And the gigantic girl at work fancies sitting on
your face?!
I'll put the kettle on!

You got a Valentine's card from your old
Scoutmaster?!
I'll put the kettle on!
He wants to show you his tent then his woggle
after?!
I'll put the kettle on!

You got punched by an ecologist? That's a green
belt!
I'll put the kettle on!
You got stuck in a car wash with Vanessa Feltz?!
I'll put the kettle on!

You asked a lady 'When's it due?' but she was just
fat!
I'll put the kettle on!
You went mountaineering in Holland, but the trip
fell flat!
I'll put the kettle on!

You got a job at the sperm bank rinsing out
specimen containers?!
I'll put the kettle on!
And Liz Truss is your new next-door neighbour?!
I'll put the kettle on!

Your son is a bellringer but he's allergic to rope?!
I'll put the kettle on!
A local farmer's accused him of fondling his
goats?!
I'll put the kettle on!

You went skydiving and your parachute broke?!
I'll put the kettle on!
You live in Stoke?!
I'll definitely put the kettle on then!

Yes, a nice cup of tea will solve everything...
Shit, I've run out of teabags!

Chav

Evil eyed, street devils
Masked, capped and unhinged
Modelling JD Sports chic but
They're not going to the gym

They're wearing their hoods up
Though it's thirty degrees
Hiding guilty, potato faces
From the CCTV

Vaping apes
Fuelled by hate
Dreaming of rape
Or scheming, plotting
To liberate purse or wallet
From handbag or pocket

The *Chaverati!*
They're the low life and arsehole of the party!

In bedrooms, stashing bags of weed
In boxes of PlayStation games
Pulling out large rolls of twenties
Hidden in socks, their ill-gotten gains

They've got friends in low places
Who're not allowed shoelaces
But get drugs to sell, blades for violence
From drones flown by these scum-pilots

Theft and robbery are elementary
Grand Theft Auto is a documentary!
Not in tea rooms or hallowed halls
But sat on curbs or graffitied walls
Waiting to strike, waiting to stripe
Knives out for one and all!

Turds of a feather
Flock together
Mock together
Shock together
Loose on mean streets
Atop bus station seats
Abusing any passer by
Who has the moral rights
To shoot these gobshites!
These wastes of life!

The *Chaverati!*
They're the low life and arsehole of the party!

Loose Women

Hello everybody! Yes, it's me!
From OnlyFans, it's Jizzy Lizzy!
You know me and what I'm like!
I'm also known as the 'National Bike!'
And people say I have the persona
Of Katie Price and Kerry Katona!

Yes, facially, I do resemble Mike Tyson
But I suck like a Dyson and fuck like a bison!
You see, when it comes to sex, I'm no novice
My snatch has seen more action than Helmand
Province!

I always wear underwear from Ann Summers
For any man that wants me, I take on all-
cummers!
Anyone with a cock, I'll show them where to put
it!
I don't charge a lot; my fanny's a bargain bucket!

My flange is an entity in its own right
It's got a blog and its own website!
It's not on *X* anymore, but used to be on *Twitter*
It's now on Instagram with my baps and my
shitter!

I'm stretched down below from years of whoring
So my minge has room if you need owt storing!
There's space for anything capacious and large!
I suppose I could take a whole canal barge!
You can come and take me out on a date
But you'd better make sure that I stay awake!
I want to talk about sex, not politics and Brexit
Cos I'm looser than a kaftan on an anorexic!

If you think I'm just an uncultured bike
We can go to an arty cinema if you like
I'll put my hand in your popcorn and grab your dick!
Cos there's nothing better than 'The Popcorn Trick'!
By the way, my favourite film is 'Taken'
And if you think I won't blow you during the trailers
Then you're very much mistaken!

And I've got mates that are just like me!
There's Beatrice, also known as 'Oral B'!
'Midnight Donna', who's kebabbed every night!
And 'Slack Alice' who's got room for two inside!

Oh, and Polly Jones, known as 'Polly Amorous'
Fucks in wheelie bins, far from glamorous!
Never faithful, never done roaming
Her vagina's half the size of Wyoming!

There's 'Luce Morals', real name Lucy
Nicknamed 'Satsuma' cos she's so juicy!
She's a little bit too fond of the fellahs!
She's wetter than a Mancunian's umbrella!

Oh, and I wrote this poem for my best mate:

Trisha wears lots of makeup
Always too much slap!
And she's shagged half of Hertfordshire
We call her the 'Watford Gap'!

She's not been in touch for a while...
To be fair, she does call a delivery guy on Uber
That comes round and takes her up the pooper!
I feel another poem coming on!

Anyway! Back to me!

Between my legs is a vag of honour
And it now looks like three-day old doner!
It's taken a battering over the years, you see
I've had more men inside me than Wembley!

Celebrities? I've had them all!
Tommy's cannon and Bobby's balls!
And friction burns from the carpet
Of that guy from A-ha, Morten Harket!

I've sucked Phil Wang's wang
And John Thompson's John Thomas!
Swallowed John Bishop's Bishop
And his spunk looked like hummus!

People call me the 'Park and Ride'
But I've got a much sweeter side
One day I'd like to find love but...
I've got a fanny like a trawlerman's glove!

Out of Practice

He'd take his kids to Eton in a flashy motor
Little princes donning tailcoats and boaters
Was he an oil magnate or tycoon? Someone rich?
Believe it or not, that man was my dentist!

Sat in the waiting room, my check-up was soon
Persian carpet on the floor, gold taps in the loo
Walls adorned by paintings by the Old Masters
It occurred to me these were fleecing bastards!

My dentist was often in the South of France
And always came back with a *healthy* tan
Somewhere between mahogany and gravy
He never looked anything but a little shady!

He whiffed of Cuban cigars and cologne
He had a flashy, gold-plated, mobile phone
He spent a lot of cash on a diamond pinky ring
And a lot of time *on* his au pair and golf swing!

But all the other dentists were just as bad!
Flaunting their wealth and what they had!
Banging on about the things they'd got!
How their wine cellars were *so* well stocked!

Twice yearly, I had check-ups and hygiene work
The treatment was painless, but the paying hurt!

They wore dental tunics that were things of beauty
But they should've been, they were made by
Gucci!

I thought: 'Are we being screwed for all they can
get?'
Cos the receptionist had diamonds around her
neck!
And I did consider asking them to cut their prices
Cos even the hygienist's watch was a bloody
Breitling!

So, we were being charged way over the odds!
They became the haves; we were the have nots!
And my dentist's three houses were over the top!
Plus, he wanted to buy a 50-foot yacht!

The parking round the back had lots of security
It was probably like the car park at United or City!
The dentists arrived in Ferraris or Aston Martins
Past we who didn't have a pot to piss or fart in!
Many of us were struggling with the cost of living
Worried we'd have to live on bread and dripping!

Then I caught one of the dentists in the street
I said 'Why do you charge so much money?'
He said the overheads are the primary cause
As he opened the door on his brand-new Porsche!
I asked why there were no better prices or deals

'Sod off, dickhead!' he said, getting behind the wheel
I said 'There's no need to be so unpleasant!'
He drove off saying: 'Eat me, you peasant!'

So I considered going to the NHS
Which I supposed might not always be the best?
But it was a fraction of what I was paying privately
And somebody's cash cow, I didn't want to be!
It wouldn't be as posh but I'd never have moaned
I'd not need to grow a money tree or apply for a loan!

But there were no places, so I had to stay longer!
And bad feelings towards the practice grew stronger
Patients asked for discounts, reductions and offers
But they just refused and kept stuffing their coffers!
The dentists got more arrogant, snobby and rude
So, us patients, on Facebook, started a group
We voiced our opinions, saying we'd not let it slide
'Cos only taxi drivers should take us for a ride!'
'We don't expect the dentists to arrive by bus!'
'But they're on a gravy train paid for by us!'

The group then agreed to take some firm action
The only way we'd get any customer satisfaction!
We started spreading the word on social media

That these rip-off merchants practised
paedophilia!
And money laundering and other heinous crimes
Planting negative things firm in people's minds!
We all went on-line and left bad reviews
'My dentist kissed me and tried to touch my
boobs!'

We could see that their little empire was falling
After we started saying their dentistry was
appalling
Siting botched fillings and iffy repairs
'My whole mouth is now a total nightmare!'
'They left our gobs in a right old mess!'
And soon, in droves, us patients left!

So, we had the last laugh, leaving en masse!
We sent the dentists off for an early bath!
And just a couple of months later
I read something in the paper
That they had officially sold up and left!
Cos they were apparently in massive debt!

But rumours were, they'd gone to hide!
After trying to open a practice in Dubai!
They went to the land of oil and sand
Where they wanted their business to expand
They'd have two floors in a new tall building

Fifty storeys high, with gold marble, floor to
ceiling!
Where they'd do rich Arab's fillings and dentures
But it proved far too expensive a venture!
Gangsters back home lent them millions of quid
With interest of a few mill added on top of it!
They paid an Arab company, a fortune in advance
But they had no planning permission! The
dentists got scammed!

The company vanished into thin air, without
trace!
The dentists would never see their money again!
When they got home, they sold everything they
had!
Cos the mob was impatient, and it wanted its
cash!
The dentists couldn't pay so they had to lie low!
After they'd all received a bullet in the post!

Three months later, a dog walker found
Some human bones sticking out of the ground!
The police examined remains of bodies in the dirt
And found a little finger poking out of the earth!
It bore a diamond, monogrammed ring; that was
it!
The end to the fucking money-grabbing dentists!

R.I.P. or R.I.P. O.F.F.?

Bovril, The Divine

Oh Bovril!
Oh Bovril!

Runny black nectar, thou art divine!
The taste of our rapture since 1889

Delectating us from where you were sent
From up on high, via Burton-on-Trent

Oh my soul, praise you, Bov almighty!
Hot beefy drink, rejoice in the taste of thee
A warm embrace as we worship at the footy
You maketh great stock and heavenly butties

Thick and salted, rightly exalted!
The extract of beef, sublime to eat!

In Heaven!
In Heaven!
We adore you the most!
In Heaven!
In Heaven!
Ambrosia on my toast!

Your glory shone, a shining star!
Within a black, red labelled jar
An apotheosis of all the spreads
Cuddling the butter, nuzzling the bread

Oh Bovril!
Oh Bovril!

Deserving of all your praise
And blessed be your name
Thy Savior that we savour
Deliver us from average flavours!

For today, Marmite, you will be cast aside!
Oh Bovril, *you* will spread for me tonight!

L

Razor cuts, tats and dungarees
Watching *Ellen* or flicking their beans
Nights of rubbing, hands are blistered
Enthusiastic Scissor Sisters!
Evenings smeared with strawberry jam
Frigging in a caravan!

Cunilingus!
Or a game of hide the fingers!
Especially in prison!
In the showers, tribadism!

Girls, I hope you're listening
Cos I can video you scissoring!
Because I have got a Steadicam
And I can film with just one hand!

You want me to take my clothes off? Great!
Why are you holding a big pair of scissors, eh?!

Pack, Man!

(California, 1982)

Hey Steve, forget about Pac Man!
We gotta pack, man!
We need to get out of this arcade!
And throw our things in a case!
Then go and catch our plane!
There's no time to waste!
No time for another game!

What, you're sensing a little friction?!
Your video gaming's become an addiction!
So, forget about these bleeping machines!
We gotta go, we gotta leave!

No pushing start to play, we're off to Spain!
Otherwise, we're gonna miss our plane!
No dodging bullets from Space Invaders!
Did you remember to get your Pesetas?
Now, in a different way, we gotta shoot!
No, we can't stop at an arcade en route!

No more jumping, climbing or zapping!
Or joystick waggling or button tapping!
Time to get away from this noise!
No more inserting frickin' coins!

Forget about Blinky, Pinky, Inky and Clyde!
You need to move your freakin' backside!
I know you've caught the pixel bug
For games like *Galaxians* and *Dig Dug*
Hurry and lose your remaining lives!
We've got to fly to literally fly!

Playing arcade games is now your life
But I won't defend ya
Love of *Defender*
If we miss our goddamned flight!

No more *Donkey Kong* or *Asteroids*
Come on now, I'm getting annoyed!
How many quarters have you put in?
Come on, my patience is wearing thin!

Shake a leg or I'll break your legs!
You really *will* see coloured lights if I see red!
They'll be no need for you to buy a telescope
Cos you'll be seeing stars if we don't hit the road!

High Score? You'll be for the high *jump* alright
If we don't make that freaking flight!
Like in *Asteroids*, you'll be in little bits
If we end up not going on this trip!
If we miss this plane tonight
You will definitely lose a life!

What do you mean, you'd rather stay?
Not sure they have video arcades in Spain?
It won't be quite like California, you say?
Gaming is better than traveling anyway?

Hey, what are those new machines they're
delivering?
People are waiting, drooling, quivering!
Wow, they are two new *Williams* ones!
One's called *Stargate*, the other's is *Robotron!*

They're forming a line already, look!
We'd better join it before the rush!
Once word gets out, this place will be packed!
Packed? We haven't finished discussing that!

Oh well...

It's 1982 and we're young and free!
San Francisco is the place to be!
Let's just enjoy the summer here!
We can still go abroad next year!

Steve, there's one thing before I forget...
Have you got any quarters left?

The Best Pest Controller

Having a problem with wasps, ants or fleas?
Then I'm your man! I'm all you need!
Because I can eject them from your home!
For I am the Master of Pest Control!

I specialise in all types of bug rescue and removal
I come to your home and with your approval
Get rid of the creepy crawlies in your house
Whether it be spider, fly, beetle or louse!

If ants are marching across your kitchen floor
And the trail leads from sugar bowl to back door
Just send me a text or give me a call!
I'll be round quick smart and sort it all!

I'll get daddy longlegs from your home
Remove the arthropods from your abode
Anything creepy or crawly, I will banish!
I'll make fleas leave and hornets vanish!

I don't stick it to stick insects or get a buzz killing
bees!
I return them all back to the wild, humanely!
Back to nature, they are all set free
I make sure they're carefully released

People seem to have heard rumours about me!
Some folk actually shout at me in the street!
They put faeces through my letterbox which is
vile!
When they hear that I'm one of those
entomophiles!
But it just means I have a love of insects!
I've a tattoo of a woodlouse on my neck!
And a butterfly down the centre of my back!
And a centipede crawling out of my crack!

I can also get rid of any rodents in your house!
Whether it be rat, shrew, vole or mouse
I'm used to dealing with vermin, you'll be glad to
hear!
I worked at the House of Commons for 15 years!

And I can remove pests from your person too!
If you're not into insects but they're into you!
I can help if you've got ants in your pants
Flies in your flies
A flea in your ear
Or you've got worms...
I can also extract voles from your holes!
But ladies, I have no truck with *Rabbits* getting
stuck!

I am a skilful and efficient bug specialist
And sometimes my methods are a bit eccentric

I can get caterpillars to crawl into a Smarties tube!
And charm any earwig with a miniature flute!

I don't have a butterfly net, just a pair of old tights
But to catch a moth or red admiral, that will
suffice
I also carefully collect creatures that people don't
like
Cos even cockroaches need love and so do those
lice!

I can pick up grasshoppers and crickets
With a fine pair of wooden chopsticks!
Get spiders to climb safely out of your bath
Dangling a piece of spaghetti, a rope for them to
catch!

I can temp beetles to move into an empty Marmite
jar
Make moths turn from the lights out to the dark
I can fence a praying mantis with a cocktail stick!
And practise Kendo with a grasshopper and a
toothpick!

I used a cotton bud to fight combative stag
beetles!
And took on a scorpion with a knitting needle!
And made naughty ladybirds change their spots!
And sprayed *Lynx* to calm down angry wasps!

I am called the *Dr Doolittle* of the insect world!
But I am *Dr Screwlittle* as I can't talk to girls!
But I can talk to the creepy crawlies!
I've had a few chats with the crickets!
And I've sung with cicadas!
And hung out with the beetles!
John, Paul, George and Ringo!
Sorry, that was just my little joke!

Anyway, call my number, any time, night or day!
I can deal with your pestilence, remove any plague
I will transport them away safely, in a humane
way
With love, consideration, respect and good grace
As God's creatures need to be treated with
kindness and love
Except for those bastard mosquitoes! They just
want your blood!

Spearmint Wino

His clothes and body stink to high heaven!
On a scale of one to ten, he's a thirty-seven!
But in a skip, he found eighty packs of Polos
Now he's got the mintiest breath of any hobo!

When the minty thrill wore off, he looked for
something harder to take!
He went into public toilets to munch on urinal
cakes!
And cos he couldn't afford to gargle with Listerine
He started drinking all the cleaner's Windolene!

After getting heavy Windolene hangovers, he quit!
Says he's staying off the cleaning products for a
bit!
He didn't eat, but he washed in McDonald's today
He's hungry but his teeth have now rotted away
Due to the booze, the meths and general decay
But he's back on the mints to keep halitosis at bay!

He may not have any clean clothes
He may not have much hope or a home
But as his mouth is always full of Polos
He's got the best breath of anyone I know!
Because he's the *Spearmint Wino!*

Whale Watching

Today, we've gone for a little swim
In the local baths which are pretty grim!
In a decrepit building that's seen better days
A testament to years of neglect and decay!

In the foyer reeking of sweat and mould
We queue behind the young and old
Push through a squeaking, rusty turnstile
Past a dead-eyed girl that never smiles!

The Ritz this place most certainly ain't!
It's been years since it's seen a lick of paint!
Into changing rooms with cracked walls and
broken doors
Last refurbished just before the Falklands War!

Us morbidly obese punters are getting undressed
We've got to move about, our doctors have
stressed!
Some of us are unemployed and some are retired
All told we should exercise before we expire!

In rusting cubicles, the removal of clothes
Where mountains of flesh are now exposed
And rolls of guts shade massive thighs
And hide our genitals from the light

This place has a strong whiff of chlorine
Which luckily masks the smell of Maureen!
She hasn't washed for three months!
You can imagine the stench from her...
'C'unt find any working lockers!'
Says Jan, pushing in her knockers
Like limpets, her costume clings
And she's got *bingo* not water wings!

Most of the ladies sprout unkempt pudenda
But this morning, Debbie shaved herself tender!
'Wait while I shove some cream in me cossie!'
'Coz now I'm sorer than a half-price prozzy!'

As Julie shouts at the top of her voice
'Anyone got a spare pound coin?'
'Ju, leave your clothes by the side!'
'They'll be safe, no one's *your* size!'

Poolside, Jumbo James lowers himself in
Puncturing the water's dark oily skin
Pukes after swallowing water through his vast
open mouth!
It takes six burly lifeguards to drag James out!

Oxtail-blue liquid fills this dank smelling hole
Where turds were once fished out with a wooden
pole!
But now they just leave them all to float

Bobbing stools forming little brown boats!
They're thinking of putting out a Tsunami
warning!
Cos Fat Sal's on the diving board this morning!
And as she thunders along it towards the pool
She knocks herself out with one of her boobs!

Gary and Yvonne are on a health kick
Despite their chain-smoking, fag habit
They descend into the pool, coughing, wheezing
Shouting: 'Bloody hell, it's fucking freezing!'

No athletes are present, just heavy strugglers
As Big Alan appears in his *budgie smugglers*
If he is the seller, there are no buyers!
And he fondly pats his huge spare tyres
Watch as the water level reaches new heights
He jumps in, proving Archimedes was right!

Tracey's had more men than a five-dollar whore!
She's always wetter than the changing room floor!
She leers at the lifeguards and gives them a wink
And she's not called 'Dick' Tracey for nothing!

Some ladies just bob about in the shallow end
A social club where they can yap to their friends
'We can't lose weight, what are we doing wrong?'
The only thing getting a workout is their tongues!

Merv the Perv swims backstroke, showing his stalker!
With his big *shark fin* sticking out of the water!
But it's OK, now that the swimmers get warned
Cos the staff play the music from the movie *Jaws*!

The whales rest by grabbing the dividers of the lanes
Then the pod lets go to battle their weight against the waves
Navigate around Mad Dan in his filthy, stained pants!
Who's starting an aqua fist fight with an ex-sailor from Gdansk!

A woman in distress is simply ignored
As dopey lifeguards, disinterested and bored
Face lit, gazing down, glued to their phones
Had we all drowned, they wouldn't have known!

Spilling out of the pool and her bikini
A semi-clad spit of Mussolini!
Linda dodders, dripping; all flab and cankles
Slips and almost breaks both of her ankles!

After ten minutes, we've all had enough!
Nearly four lengths have been quite tough!

Haul ourselves out, then a wet waddle to get
washed
Now we're all starving, so we're ready for some
scoff!

In showers with buttons you have to keep pushing
An old, shaky man resembling Peter Cushing
Stares intently at Mandy with goggling eyes
He's pretty damned partial to lumpy, puckered
thighs!

These are not sights I can easily forget!
Burn out my eyes out with a cigarette!
Cos Mandy washes her creases to remove the
sweat
And her arse weighs more than a jumbo jet!

We wobble in, shouting, banging locker doors
And stomping and dripping on a dirty wet floor
I'll take pictures of us and hang them on the wall!
Prints of Whales is what they'll be called!

We've washed and dried our bits and chuffs
Now wrapped in towels not big enough
We're all in danger of indecent exposure
And nobody wants to see *us* bending over!

Sodden costumes are now chucked in bags
Cos we want to get out as soon as we can!

Sue's using the only working hair dryer
Shouting 'I wasn't in long. I was too bloody tired!'

We funnel out to the exit gate queue
With a missing sock or an extra shoe
Chelle asks Janice if needs the loo
'It's OK love, I went in the pool!'

In the foyer with damp, frizzy hair
Tracey and Sal are already sat there
Heads in a massive trifle she brought from home
Faces covered with cream, not for the first time,
you know!

Gary shambles in, crumpled and covered in sweat
Asks why the leisure centre doesn't sell cigarettes
Yvonne says she's continuing her new health
streak
She plans to eat half an apple sometime next
week!

But we now have pleasure in the leisure centre!
When the vending machine spills it treasure!
Twix, Snickers, KitKat and Mars
Stuffing our faces, shuffling out to our cars

Rita's got a meal waiting at home
But it's not a hot lunch, it's very cold!

Five minutes until *Ben and Jerry's* are thawed before
Six tubs are voraciously spooned into her maw!

We're glad we visited the baths, it was a laugh!
We have earned our lunchtime doner kebab!
Then, in front of the telly, we'll sink into sofas
Mauling pizza, remotes and console controllers
And apologies to the staff, if we made a mess!
The changing rooms are trashed and very wet!
If you think we're not coming back, have no fear!
We'll see you all again, same time, next year!

Mange Toucan

There is an idiom 'Horses for Courses'
But the French take it too far!
Ils mangent du cheval pour le déjeuner et le dîner
And here, was a dinner plate the fate of Shergar?!

The French eat horse as a main dish in restaurants
To me, that's a non-starter! Ha-Ha!
And they have pig's trotters and frog's legs
And that raw mince dish, beef tartare!

In Korea, they have dog for their tea!
While Cambodians eat fried spiders!
In Iceland, they have whale blubber
Would you want any of that lot inside ya?!

Let Britain compete with our own weird meats!
What odd meals though, would we consume?
Let's eat 'Owl and Mash' or 'Badger on a Bap'!
Oh, in Gloucestershire, they already do?!

Anyway, I'm going to go veggie because
Eating animals gives me such sorrow
You've already made me a bacon sandwich?
OK, maybe I'll start tomorrow!

Binfluencer

Around eight o'clock every Sunday night
I go and put the bins out down the drive
I'm out of the door, bang on time
And grab the bin from around the side

A check to see nothing within is banned
Then on the handle, two hands
Carefully feeling the hefty weight
I tilt and push it through the gate

I see curtains twitch and move
And pairs of eyes, peeping through!
Neighbours want to know what I've picked
Recycling, garden or the 'normal' bin

As I wheel it down, they're watching me
They rely on me to take the lead!
It's not a time for indecision!
They're waiting for my bin decision!

I feel their gaze and I'm exposed
As I check the lid is firmly closed
I leave the bin down by the curb
By a dead rat and large dog turd

My fellow street dwellers understand
Their fate is solely in my hands!
They break cover, following my direction!
Then, all proceed to copy my selection!
Nodding and quickly scuttling back inside
I'd like to chat, but they've never got time!

If I put out the incorrect bin
My neighbours would flip their lids!
Silver, Brown, Green or Black
Whatever the colour, I've got their backs!

I'm the most important man in the street!
Everyone that lives here looks up to me!
And I can always hold my head up high
Cos the bins are out by quarter past nine!

On my forty-fifth birthday, my mother said
'I'm so proud of you, you're a leader of men!'
'Thank you, Mum! I'm an influencer!'
'More than that, son, you're a Binfluencer!'

I'm having a bin party next weekend!
You're all invited, bring your friends!
We'll celebrate our refuse and recycling wins!
And I'll serve drinks on top of the bins!

We'll have a *wheelie* good time!
You're not coming? You're busy that night?
Maybe next time you won't *refuse!*
Bin good talking to you!

Am I sane? You have your doubts!
You might say that the jury's out!
But, by 8pm, so are the bins!!!!

Dating An Anorexic

At the Anorexic Speed Dating night
There were incredibly slim pickings!
I went along as I wanted to meet
The skinniest women in Britain!

I was looking for a slender lady
A wafer thin, scrawny piece!
I like girls that are very slight, ones
That make supermodels look obese!

But the doorman wouldn't let me in!
Said I had to be much thinner!
And he said that he, did not believe
I had missed too many dinners!

I said 'I've an eating disorder - I'm half bulimic!'
'What is that then?' he said
I said 'I do all the binge eating but I
Haven't got round to throwing up yet!'

I didn't think he looked convinced
So I just slipped him a tenner!
He said 'You've met the entry requirements!'
And so, he allowed me to enter

Inside, emaciated daters wearing badges
Were herded around like cattle
They looked like a skeleton army
Ready to go into battle!

I got a few funny looks
As I sat and took my seat!
Us men opposite ten thin girls
With five minutes to chat to each

There was Jane who was an electrician
When she entered, she lit up the room!
With upright, coarse, wiry hair
She looked like a caretaker's broom!

With a flat face of sallow, yellowing skin
There was a girl there called Annaleise
With her square head on a pale thin body
She looked like a cocktail stick with cheese!

The bar only had Diet Coke and was pricey
But I was told that the buffet was free
And was disappointed with the anorexic's banquet
It was just lots of tap water and celery!

I had an instant connection with a doe-eyed girl
Went we talked, something just hit me!
After five minutes were up, *I* was as well!
Cos I was sporting a colossal stiffy!

I'm taking her out but can only just make her out!
I'm seeing her but can only just about see her!
And she's not called 'Thin Lizzy' or 'Bony Em'
Or 'Anna Rexic'! She's actually called 'Lena'!

The first time I went around to her house
I noticed she didn't have any mirrors
I thought she might be a vampire!
Well, she hates garlic, so that figures!

She's got no cooker or microwave
She's got no use for them you see!
Cos one thing I know about her is
The last thing she wants to do is eat!

Another thing I noticed in her home
She doesn't own any bathroom scales
She doesn't see herself the way others do
And thinks she looks like some kind of whale!

I do like the malnourished look!
And they say opposites attract!
She looks like she's been rescued from a famine!
And I am just basically fat!

Her hair is very brittle
And self-confidence is low
And in the summer, she wears a scarf
Cos she's always, always cold!

We went out shopping for clothes
Said I'd treat her to a new dress
But she says size zero's too big!
She can only wear XXXXS!

She's really so incredibly scrawny
But nothing peaks my interest
Like bones that poke through the skin
And a low body mass index!

With a crooked head on bony shoulders
She looks like a human coat hanger!
You think that would put me off but
She's my tambourine and I want to bang her!

She hates me using words that are also foods
I can't say things like 'jam' or 'crumbs'
And go on a 'date' or call her 'sugar' or 'honey'
But I can tell you she likes 'nuts' and 'plums'!

I think she must be body dysmorphic!
She hates her looks, but I don't one bit!
Cos I can play the xylophone on her bones
From her spine right round to her ribs!

She got dolled up and wanted to impress
And looked like a corpse wrapped in a dress!
I'm five times her weight, it has to be said!
I'd estimate she's four stone, wringing wet!

I jumped on her in bed, in a moment of lust!
I flattened her, and instantly her ribs turned to
dust!

So, I sent her pancaked body to A&E!
After a year of surgery, she's recovered and we
Are now together as solid as a rock!
Our sex life's great but she's always on top!

I really love the bones of her!
And I can see them quite clearly
I can imagine what she'd look like dead!
She looks like she's already there, nearly!

I wonder how she'll look in forty years' time?
Possibly one of those wizened old crones?
Or Albert Steptoe, Zelda from *Terrahawks*
Or maybe something out of *Game of Thrones*?

So, do I recommend dating an anorexic?
Yes, I have to say that it's great!
For even if we go for dinner, I'm still on a winner
Cos she'll never steal the chips from my plate!

Rocket Man

On the fateful night of November 5th
Kevin Jones did something very stupid!
He tried to impress his mates but went too far!
He lit a Roman candle and shoved it up his arse!

He thought he would fly through the sky!
On a ride, high on Bonfire Night!
Singing Elton John's tune as he flew
But instead, his arsehole was blown in two!

They recovered his arms, his head and his legs
So they could get him buried and put him to rest
Friends told his family that time would heal
But his ringpiece is still missing, somewhere in a field!

Stuffed

I'm fit for nothing
Cos I'm fit to burst!
I've really overindulged
My stomach really hurts!

Today, I was such a social butterfly!
And everything seemed to involve food!
I had breakfast, lunch, and dinner meetings
And refusing Afternoon Tea would've been rude!

I met people for elevenses and supper too!
It feels like I've now swallowed a planet!
No wonder I've gained ten pounds today!
I'm a human dustbin! A total gannet!

You'd have thought that I'd been force fed!
Gorging on what I like, everything in sight!
I've chucked too much scran down my neck!
I did the opposite of a hunger strike!

I've been scoffing it, troughing it
It's all ended up in my maw!
Not spilling it or dropping it
No crumbs did hit the floor!

And, for charity, I sat in a baked bean filled bath!
I ate all the beans on an eight-foot piece of toast!
A human Pacman, scoffing everything in my path!
And then I went to me mum's for a big Sunday
Roast!

Which one of the Mr Men am I? Mr Greedy?!
Well, I *do* resemble him, I'll admit!
I have the big grin, a similar shape to him
And I'm also the same shade of pink!

I smelt all the nice food with my porcine snout!
Whatever I could grab; seasonal or artisanal
Before demolishing, polishing off and pigging out!
I was greedier than a Labrador and a Blackpool
Seagull!

I can hear bubbling, burbling, gurgling and
popping!
And other strange noises from within!
Like the Hulk, my shirt is about to burst!
I think that my buttons are about to go ping!

Cos my poor stomach's now so very angry
There's a chance I might actually be dying!
My gut's pissed off, too much Banoffee and
Biscoff!
And I shouldn't have shoved more Shepard's Pie
in!

I felt the worse for wear after the chocolate eclairs
Normally, gorging on sweet things won't harm me
Cos I'm a professional pudding eater; a real
deserter!
Though I've never actually been in the army!

Some friends came round, which didn't help
either!
I sat and scoffed ice cream with Ben and Jerry!
Then me and Rita ate three bags of Malteesers!
And I ate Chocolate Oranges with Terry!

My bloating and fullness subsided a bit
Eating nowt for ten minutes, I felt better!
But then, me and Vaughan, ate bowls of popcorn!
And polished off a whole Viennetta with Emma!

It feels like I've devoured entire worlds!
And swallowed a whole universe too!
Mr Creosote! You were an amateur!
Compared to what I've just consumed!

I feel like the size of a retail park!
Or at least, a small shopping mall!
I've vommed a bit, but it's not relieved it
I still look like I'm smuggling beach balls!

So now, I'm feeling like a bag of shite!
And I've only got myself to blame!

I should've had greens and nutritious things!
Rather than just barrowfuls of beige!

I'm definitely not feeling too clever!
It feels like I could just croak soon!
There's something going on in there!
Like the fish fingers are trying to poke through!

Shit! I think I'm gonna give birth!
Quick someone, get me the stirrups!
I don't think it's gonna be twins!
It's quints, quads or at least triplets!

Hurry! Get me to the Maternity Unit!
Tell the midwife, a turd baby's coming!
Cos it may be a load of shit, I know, but
I'll be reunited with my pies and puddings!

The Overdressed

Look the part, wherever you're heading!
Always dress up like you're off to a wedding!

Don't be a mess, try and look your best!
When you go out to the Tesco Express!

Going to Timpson's for new shoelaces?
Get dolled up, like you're off to the races!

Dropping your car off for a service at the local
garage?
Clothe yourself like you're in the King's royal
carriage!

Wear that posh new bra that shows off your tits!
So you can *nip* out for milk from the local Londis!

You just don't need to be a scruffy shopper!
When you can visit Primark in your best clobber!

Dressed to kill, like you're off to the BAFTAs!
Though you're only buying bin bags from ASDA!

Look like you're going to Wimbledon for the tennis!
When really, it's for a check-up at the dreaded dentist!

Spend three hours solid, primping and preening!
Just to go and collect your dry cleaning!

Girls, wear your shiny new Jimmy Choos!
To go to B&M or fill up with fuel!

Boys, you can cut a dash in a silk cravat!
Then, catch a bus to the football match!

So, I say to you all! Dress to impress!
Join me and be... *The Overdressed!*

Excuse me, I've got to go!
To don a top hat and a cloak
As I'm off to... Stoke!

Wind Power

Listen Doctor, I know it's bit absurd
But I think you must have misheard!
Viagra? I don't want pills to be a *better lover!*
I want pills to be a *better guffer!*

You see, compared to my mates, I feel inferior
Cos they've got much more blowy posteriors!
Like the countries of Malta, Malaysia and Gambia
They've got no wind power! And I don't either!

When my friends and I let rip in the pub
I'm embarrassed, cos my farts have no umph!
You see, it's just not at all to my satisfaction
To have such a terribly weak pump action!

I want to make the walls of buildings shake!
Like I'm right in the middle of an earthquake!
It's a super guff that I want to bake!
Doc, are there any meds that I can take?
If I was cured, I think I'd change my name
To 'Windy Miller', 'Farting Martin' or 'Gassius
Clay'!

I want to make children's hair stand on end!
Make people run and warn their friends!

About the approaching bottom hurricane!
And to check their insurance is up to date!
I'll tell people to take cover until it passes!
Hide in their cellars and batten down the hatches!
With the power to pull up trees and damage
houses!
From the anal tornado in the back of my trousers!

Doctor, I've tried the prunes and beans
Eggs, cabbage and other dietary means
Can you please tell me what to do?
Because I just keep following through!

It's all to no avail you see!
My botty gust is just a breeze!
I want it to tear through the air!
Cause a storm from my derriere!

Doctor, I hope you will kindly accord
Because I want to direct a fart with force!
Be able to blow a ship off its course!
Knock over a cow or even a horse!

Then, socially, I won't feel disowned
And all the ladies will jump my bones!
If I can produce something potent from my ass
They'd say, 'Now there goes a real man!'

I'm in your hands; you can change my world!
I could then maybe meet a really nice girl!
I'd not need to use an app like Tinder
If you could put an amp up my sphincter!

Doctor, do you think you can help me?
I know it's not really a priority
I don't want to waste the NHS's time
But can you aid me with my plight?

I want a gale force wind when I fart!
Have weather presenters put me on their charts!
Doctor, I would be famous at last!
So, please, please, please make my bottom blast!!

Almost Famous

When I was on the rise to the top
When I was giving it all I got
When I was climbing up that greasy pole
Eyes on the prize, mind on the goal
When I had to crawl, scrabble and fight
To reach the peak at those dizzying heights
When I wanted to see my name in lights
When I longed for fame, that big star prize
Reminiscing about when I'd almost made it
The memories of a struggle that's quickly fading

When I was on the brink of something exciting
Before they decided my teeth needed whitening
And while I was there, I should bleach my anus!
I miss those Halcyon Days before I was famous

When people didn't photograph me in the bath
Or try to watch me having a slash
Didn't care what I thought, bought, and how I
looked
Who I kissed, hugged or who I fucked

When journo's mud wasn't flung in my direction
When I wasn't slated in the arty culture sections
When I was one of the masses, one of the punters

When I didn't have to avoid autograph hunters
When I could slob around all day, being a sciver
When my YouTube channel had few subscribers
When I was still a nobody and totally obscure
When I was nearly happy and moderately poor

Nobody asking for gossip from my friends
Or taking pics of me through a long lens
No one looking in my shopping trolley
No one serving, random, verbal volleys!

No having to go to those showbiz parties
Where pills were handed out like Smarties
Where me, and the stars, a real Who's Who!
Did long lines of white powder in the loo!

When I didn't get red carpet treatment
And birthday cards from Paul Heaton
When I didn't have influence and get my own way
When I hadn't got a Knighthood or been into
space

Before I was worshipped as much as the Pope
Before I had climbed over that velvet rope
Before the fancy restaurants and private clubs
I ordered from laminated menus in shitty pubs

When I bought my own tickets for the footy or
gigs
And I wasn't gifted holidays, cars and other things
When I wasn't paid a fortune to make films or
write novels
When I didn't have threesomes with Scandinavian
models!
When there wasn't champagne in First Class to
enjoy
When I had to queue for hours with the hoi polloi
When I wasn't invited round by the Beckhams and
Rooneys
When I wasn't followed by randy young groupies

It seemed like I was having an amazing time!
But I realised my life was a bucket of shite!
Newspaper stories, crazy fans and zero privacy!
Mental health issues like panic attacks or anxiety!
Stalkers, forming relationships and public
scrutiny!
Drug problems, fake friends and the paparazzi!
And paranoia, depression, isolation and fear!
Insecurity, exhaustion, being hassled and jeered!

And just when I thought I might give fame up!
A chance that most people don't get, came up!
I got to kick Russell Brand square in the balls!
So maybe fame isn't all that bad after all!

Roger The Bodger

He'll come round almost straight away
And he says that no job is too small!
He's always free and he's very cheap
There's nowt he won't tackle at all!

He'll attempt any heating or electrical task
But he's not even qualified or trained!
And he's highly rated on *CheckATrade*
He wrote the reviews and they're fake!

He'll try to fix your leaky taps or pipes
But your plumbing will still be knackered!
He'll create a water feature in your house
Like that one they had at Old Trafford!

I think he's from another age of human evolution!
He resembles a Neanderthal or Neolithic man!
He frowns and grunts as he gets to work
With rudimentary tools from the back of his van

He looks puzzled but carries on regardless
As he clatters, batters and hammers
He makes a few mistakes, he'll admit, cos
He's just no good at practical matters!

His services are scrawled in biro on a napkin
And this 'business card' lists 'interior lighting'
'Yes, I've had a few fires, I won't be a liar!'
'Because I'm just a bit unlucky with wiring!'

He never went to college, he doesn't have much knowledge!
Heating gets the beating of him, electricity's a mystery!
When fixing his neighbour's garden lights, it all turned to shite!
Put it this way, their koi carp are now history!

He installed a new boiler for the Taylor's
In their beautiful Victorian abode
And eight people are still missing!
After he blew up half of the road!

He tried to extend his brother's kitchen
Said he'd do it in two days flat!
But he knocked down a load bearing wall
Now the house has partly collapsed!

He did some tiling at my neighbour's house
His enthusiasm never lacked or diminished
The tiles were marked, broken and raised
And that was *after* he'd finished!

I hired him once to put up some shelves
But he just made huge holes in the walls!
Most of the room resembled Swiss Cheese!
Like giant mice had eaten the plasterboard!
But now people know his name!
And he's always wanted to be famous!
He's appeared on a BBC TV show!
Heard of it? It's called *Rogue Traders*!

Sometimes he doesn't use his van
He just turns up on a horse!
And for lunch he has baked beans
Sat around a campfire of course!
I'm not saying he's a cowboy or owt like that
But he has been known to wear a Stetson hat!
The sound of his spurs lets you know he's coming
As he arrives to ruin your heating or plumbing!

He's not a painter, electrician or a fencer
Because really, he's just a big Frank Spencer!
Completely accident prone and totally inept
A more useless tradesman you could not get!
He's got to be the worst handyman in Britain!
And that's up against some stiff competition!

This handyman is unhandy, man!
As practical as a bottomless watering can!

If you're looking for a useless electrician or
plumber
I'll give you his details, I've got his new number
The prison officers will pass a message on
Just let him know what you want done
He'll call you back or send you a mail
In a couple of weeks, he'll be out on bail!

He says he knows what he's doing!
He doesn't need to look it up!
He'll keep hammering and screwing!
His work's guaranteed... to fuck it up!

Yaffle

Hands behind back, looking over his specs
He ambles in an approved fashion like King
Charles
Resembling that Professor Yaffle from *Bagpuss*
Though he's a woodpecker and has no arms

Talking to others in gentle tones
Arms at the rear, clasped hands
Walking like a Cambridge Don
Doing what is called a *Regal Stance*

In an old, woollen cardigan
Under a beige, Gabardine mac
He's intently browsing antiques
And perusing bric-a-brac crap

Does he want to look like Liam Gallagher?
Or a salesman surprising browsers unaware?
A police inspector questioning suspects?
Or is he walking behind a funeral cortege?

Perhaps he just wants to be tied up!
Like that hostage guy, Terry Waite!
Or he fancies himself as Houdini
And maybe he's trying to escape?

I could have got this chap wrong!
Maybe he doesn't want to be fettered!
He wants freedom to look over his glasses at us
And make us feel like he's somehow better!

Oh, hang on though, he's got blood!
All over the seat of his jeans!
I heard, his botty got drilled last night
By a group of old randy queens!

So *that's* why he's walking like that!
He's got an extremely painful posterior!
He will still walk funny, and we can laugh
But it doesn't stop him from looking superior!

Fifty Shades of Graham

I know a local, middle-aged man
Who's very proud of his all-over tan
He spends two hours every single day
Dabbing his whole body with fence paint!
He goes by the name of Graham Hock
It's his fault when B&Q are out of stock!
Cos he's a raider of the exterior woodcare section
But his body's got six years of weather protection!

Burnt Umber, Walnut or *Deep Mahogany*
Help to transform his physiognomy
Harvest Gold is a shade he finds quite racy
It would have made Dale Winton look quite pasty!
He's the man with the tan that stands out the
most
And makes Donald Trump look as white as a
ghost!

His very loyal mate, Ron Seal
Shares his passion with such zeal
Cos he loves fence paint too, with a fervour
They have nights in with a couple of cans...
Of wood preserver!

Graham's getting ready now as he's out tonight
He always makes sure his shading's right!

Tops up his tan with his best fence brushes
Blob, blob, dabbing on the finishing touches

This evening, he's flying solo, out on the tiles
He'll be the most tanned bloke by a country mile!
He's now a bit of a celebrity in this town
Everyone wants to see his latest shade of brown
He often gets stopped and selfies are taken
And he *has* been mistaken for a Jamaican!
Tonight, he'll get plenty of admiring glances
And he's planning on tickling a few girls' fancies!

And so, the ladies flock to him and get in line
He's stained more than a few lassies in his time!
And it's true to say, Graham resembles a shed!
The girls don't mind, they like a bit of wood in
bed!

I suppose he would be the first to admit
He's never really been a mahogany monogamist
But once he had a steady girlfriend on his arm
Someone who fell for his timbered charms
Her name was Koo Prinol and liked the cut of his
jib
She liked a real man - and he was 'non-drip'
She said, 'I like a man with a tan!'
'Want my bloke to look like oak!'
'But if darker, even better!'
'I fancy guys that look like leather!'

But she caught him with other ladies!
She said, 'You are warped and shady!'
Cos with many girls, Graham had fiddled
He infected her with woodworm! She was riddled!

But even though he was so besotted
She still told him to go and get knotted!

Tomorrow, he's going to change things up!
He's decided on a fresh new look!
This time, it'll be a much lighter tan
He's going to be the colour of sand!
Changing to this shade will take him hours
But after, he'll be beiger than a pensioner's
trousers!
And he may then be the hue of camels...
But he'll always look like one of your fence panels!

Deluded

It seems the whole world has concluded
That I am totally and utterly deluded!
I thought I deserved a portion of fame
Served on a bed of critical acclaim!

I thought I had some talent
But it's apparent, I haven't!
I thought I was born star-shaped
Turns out, I'm just half-baked!

No prospect of gigs, auditions or roles
Just the promise of the bloody dole
I'm so lazy; a persona non-grafter!
And I'm no singer, dancer or actor
But at least there's always... X Factor!

Middle Class Blues

My shea butter bubble bath doesn't last long
enough!
My queso de Cabrales doesn't taste strong
enough!
And my scented candles just don't pong enough!
These are Middle Class Blues

Avocados and Asian pears are filling the kitchen
bin!
With last night's porterhouse, it's all starting to
stink!
And the cleaner's gone AWOL, she hasn't come in!
These are Middle Class Blues

I'm jealous of my best friend's new Louboutin
shoes!
I nearly didn't get Tom and Olivia in the best
school!
And there are *so* many leaves in the swimming
pool!
These are Middle Class Blues

Olivia's taught Mandarin but she always
complains!
My newest blouse got wine and truffle-oil stained!

I can't find any Farrow and Ball Hague Blue paint!
These are Middle Class Blues

Burned my mouth eating baked camembert!
I bought an expensive dress and nobody stared!
Leant naked on the Aga and singed my public
hair!
These are Middle Class Blues

I sent Hubby shopping, he does what he's told to!
He reported there was no swordfish in
WholeFoods!
The weekend's ruined! And we're now out of tofu!
These are Middle Class Blues

Waitrose had no quinoa or any bok choy!
Had to nip to Sainsbury's with the hoi polloi!
Otherwise, I'd be stuck with just wretched Savoy!
These are Middle Class Blues

There's no star anise left on the pantry shelf!
And I'm low on tahini, seaweed and kelp!
Ocado doesn't get here til five, so that's no help!
These are Middle Class Blues

My Range Rover is now nearly six months old!
And today, NONE of my art even got sold!
And at lunch, my Gazpacho was not even cold!
These are Middle Class Blues

I fancy my yoga teacher; he looks like Jacob Rees
Mogg!
But I don't think he fancies this mumsy old bod!
And I farted quite violently doing the downward
dog!
These are Middle Class Blues
(And I get the farties during Pilates!)

My hairstylist's booked up, I can't get a trim!
The gardener's late and I can't get hold of him!
And I nearly had to bring in my own wheelie bins!
These are Middle Class Blues

My Mulberry silk skirt was put on a boil wash!
It *was* full length now it's more like a half!
And the dogs have torn up all my chiffon scarves!
These are Middle Class Blues

Not much this week to give me good cheer
Don Giovanni's sold out for Saturday, I hear!
And Tuscany is apparently overcrowded this year!
These are Middle Class Blues

When I think about my life there are things I find
upsetting
There are some choices I find myself regretting
Like I can't believe I bought a toaster without a
bagel setting!
These are Middle Class Blues

But other things can bring on the tears
When I think of some of my greatest fears
Like our children will grow up only average skiers!
These are Middle Class Blues

Off to Henley tomorrow but I can't find my
boater!
And my cats have shat in my Prada loafers!
And I saw our elderly neighbours playing strip
poker!
After the day I've had, tonight I won't be sober!
It'll be Pinot G, Downton and Mumsnet on the
sofa!
These are Middle Class Blues
These are Middle Class Blues

Calmer and Karma

Today, I went for a stroll to lift my spirits
I communed with nature and all within it
I had a deep sense of serenity within me
In a state of inner peace and tranquillity

A profound sensation of stillness and calm
When I saw Piers Morgan slip and break his arm
Then the sun on my face felt like nature's kiss
As I passed an estate agent falling off a bridge

From a tree, a blackbird sang me a little tune
As Simon Cowell was buggered with a wooden
spoon
And I was suddenly met with a delightful breeze
While a baseball bat connected with a traffic
warden's knees

I had a lovely walk through a woodland dell
As a tax inspector was pushed down a well
My spirits were awoken and lifted higher
Watching Katie Hopkins eaten by a tiger

Above, a wonderful rainbow nature then brought
With angry lobsters in Richard Branson's shorts

I felt humble like when Jesus was a carpenter
Seeing Gregg Wallace run over by a combine
harvester

I thought peace and harmony was restored
But the rain came and it started to pour
It turns out nothing will be like it oughta
Til Russell Brand is hung, drawn and quartered!

Do Ya Wanna Buy My Car?

Thanks for coming to look at my car
This motor's been an absolute star!
It's never, ever put a wheel wrong!
And lucky you, it's going for a song!

It's been honestly superb, even sublime!
Have a look round it, take your time!

Yes, there's a little wear and tear
But it's never broken down, I swear!
The bodywork's still in pretty good shape
Just ignore all the little bits of tape!

The brake lights are broken at the back?
I'll knock a bit off the price for that!
The tyres are bald and quite flat?
Yeah, they *are* a little bit Kojak!

Want to have a look inside?
Oh, the door opens *most* of the time!
You just have to pull it hard!
Or occasionally use a crowbar!
Just be careful how and where you sit
Yes, there *is* a slight smell of shit...

Ignore any stains you find on the dash!
There's bound to be the odd scrape and scratch!

You say the back smells like a rotting fox?
Well, at least it's better than the glove box!

In the footwell, there's a brown pool?
Oh, that'll be some liquid stool!
Just forget that it's actually poo!
Maybe imagine it's some Oxtail soup!

There's a funny thing under the seat?
That's just a strip of old doner meat!
You think it's covering a crack in the floor?
Chewing gum's plugging a hole in the door?

I'm trying to cover a multitude of sins?
And looks like a 'Cut and Shut' you think?
Well, you'll get two cars for the price of one!
Better snap it up then before it's gone!

Would you like to take it for a drive?
What? You say you'd be risking your life?!
It's a death trap?! What do you mean?!
I should just come clean?! OK, I'll concede...

That it handles like a three-wheel van!
With grip like a man with no hands!
It's got keyless entry though! The doors don't lock!
And the VIN does seem to have been scrubbed off!

The absorbers are a bit of a shock!
And there *are* a few miles on the clock!
The equivalent of the Earth to Saturn!
With two previous careful owners: Prince Phillip
and Richard Hammond!

Yes, there's a touch of rust!
The brake pads have turned to dust!
Yeah, them's the brakes!
You press your foot down and pray!
But it passed its MOT...once!
And the car still runs...out of petrol!

And yes, the indicators blink
When you shift into fifth!
The steering *is* bit hit and miss!
It often veers right a bit!
But it gets much worse
When you try and reverse!
Then it stutters and whines
And occasionally catches fire!

You don't think the headlights work, you say?
Easily solved, just drive in the day!
You heard squeaking? Oh, that's just the mice!
They live in the bodywork, they're included in the
price!
What about the service history?
Well, it's all a bit of a mystery!

So I can't help you with your enquiry
Cos the log book's emptier than a hermit's diary!
You're not going to take it for a spin?
Because it's a rusting, hulk of tin?
You don't want a quick burn up the road?
You're not that brave, you're not that bold?

I assure you it's safe and not a death trap!
If you keep it steady and don't go too fast!
Just keep it under ten miles an hour!
That as fast as it goes - it's got no power!

What do you mean it's a pile of crap?!
I'd be better off taking it for scrap?!
Where are you going?! Are you not keen?!
Have I put you off or something?!

Wait!
£500 and it's all yours!
What do I take you for?!

I'm not budging! I'm not some kind of door mat!
OK, four-fifty and I'll throw in the floor mats!

No? You drive a hard bargain, mate!
I think maybe we should negotiate!
Where are you going? You can't walk away?!
Okay, Okay, Okay, Okay!
What if I give you £50 to take it away?

The Seagull

Under marshmallow pillows and cotton wool, I
glide
Over dancing light on the blue below, I dive, I
climb

I'm a lone fool, having my fun
Salty air cools as I turn to the sun
I soar, I caw
The flock arrives at my side
On another thermal, we ride
As one, we cry

We coast then we rise together
High-flying birds of a feather
I feel I can't climb anymore and yet...
Ascend further before a steep bank left

We play, we chase
Over the crashing, rolling waves
Wheeling and swooping
Coasting and looping

Two hundred feet above the turquoise and green
The tang of the briny sea
Expending energy, I am hungry!

I spot something from way up here!
I'm looking at a woman walking on the pier!
She's got a baguette the size of a bazooka!
So I dive down on her like a *Stuka!*
She drops it when I buzz her head!
She takes cover as I take off and scoff half her
bread!
I stuff it down me in a couple of gulps
But I am nowhere close to being full!

I spy a guy with a pie! I think it's a Pukka!
Right, I'm going to rob that dozy fucker!
I peck at his head and make it bleed!
Witness, white winged, daylight robbery!
As the bloke is now sat, getting first-aid
He's watching me eat his pie, three yards away!

And look at those chips that young lad's got!
I'm gonna claw at him til he drops the lot!
Which he duly does and the flock swoops down
It's a group fish supper in the middle of the town!

Soon, I'm on the counter in the kebab house
The staff try to swipe and shoo me out!
I leave with stolen doner and eat it alfresco
Perched on the roof of the nearby Tesco!

Tourists and locals are intimidated by our gang
From sky and roof, we're surveying your scran!

None of you can just eat outside and relax
We're ready to swoop and attack your snacks!

We will taunt you humans as you're helpless!
We can hurt you, but you can't hurt us!
You know we can be as aggressive as we like!
Harm us and you'll get a five grand fine!
You must give in and take it on the chin!
The law as it stands lets us *always* win!
I'm off now to do my *gull friend* on top of the
bins!

The Ghosts in the Machines

Ever wondered why vending machines break?
Why people think they're such a real pain?
Why they often dispense the wrong thing or nowt?
Why you have to kick them or give them a clout?
Well, it might just be because of me!
Cos I am the *Ghost in the Vending Machine!*

When the slot's jammed or your coins rejected
Or you don't get out what you've selected
When you're waiting for those spirals to turn
Delivering the Quavers or Twix that you yearn
Your Bounty is teetering but won't quite drop
Well, it's me that makes those coils just stop!

I dream about hiding behind a Cadbury's Boost!
My decapitated head would materialise, 'Boo!'
Then my headless body would appear from
around the back!
Making you jump out of your skin reaching in for
your KitKat!
But alas, I think you'll just have a heart attack!

Instead, I make you angry and bash the glass!
Headbutt it and shout 'You robbing twat!'
Boot the machine and rock it from side to side!
When you realise you've been taken for a ride!

But I'm not the only wraith to spook such spaces
I'll introduce my mates who haunt other places...

I am the *Ghost in the Washing Machine!*
Preventing your clothes from getting clean
Sobbing in the drum as your clothes spin round
You'll see they've shrunk when you take them out!

I am the *Ghost in the Fruit Machine!*
Your losing streak is all down to me!
You'll never win the jackpot with *me* inside!
I'll give you lemons alright but not in a line!

I am the *Ghost in the Sewing Machine!*
Unseen on TV in the *Great British Sewing Bee!*
Or hiding inside your brand new Singer!
I'm the reason you sewed your own finger!

I am the *Ghost in the Condom Machine!*
In metal boxes on walls in gent's lavatories
Lads, in the nightclub after you've copped off
I'm the reason your pack of johnnies didn't drop!
And you wasted that shiny two quid
So, you just had to go bareback, kid!

We are the *Ghosts in the Machines!*
Just call a priest if you want us to leave!
They'll perform an exorcism if you feel irked
But wouldn't life be boring if everything worked?

The Loping Opener

Perfect conditions for cricket, this afternoon!
On this fine Saturday in the middle of June
With a slight breeze in glorious weather
In a well-healed village in deepest Cheshire
Ladies in the pavilion with Prosecco and cream
teas
Waiting for Tom Cavendish: *The Wizard of the
Crease!*

In the changing room, he's in the zone
Hair is waxed, a splash of cologne
His teeth are dazzling like the whites he's got on
Both are brighter than an Oxbridge Don!
Breath is checked and eyebrows smoothed
He knows what he's got to go out and do!
Pulling on his trademark vest pullover
'I am the man!' he chants over and over!

He's prepped, primed and now it's showtime!
That distinctive, long, bounding stride
Walking proudly out, almost running
The bowler gulps, he knows what's coming!

Tom reaches the crease and swings his bat
Then dons his helmet as the crowd claps
Affording a glance to his adoring fans as
The umpire shouts 'Play' to start the match

Tom's always the first of the eleven
And soon, he's notched up seventy-seven!
Bottle after bottle, getting through the booze
The ladies are admiring the captain's every move!
Imagining spicy nights with him between the sheets
Polite applause becomes wolf-whistles and shrieks!

The usual muted clapping from the jealous men
Conflicted by having him in the team with them
'He's an attention-seeking, poncey, flash git!'
'But he's *so* gifted, our team always wins!'
See the sighing men wait for their turn!
See the sighing women wait for *their* turn!
As the flannelled Adonis is stood at the crease
Whacks home another couple of sixes with ease
He raises his helmet as a century is reached
Could he do the same at that age with the ladies?!

The ladies are glad their men are not near though
So they can focus on their battling, batting hero
The few that haven't had him, wish they had
And the ones that have, want a return match!
And so, Tom never really needs to oil his bat
He's always got plenty of volunteers for that!

Always going for a boundary, lines he shouldn't
cross!
Like sleeping with the chairman's wife, Anita
Ross!
Two hours after, he had the club secretary, Amy
Deering!
They certainly had something to talk about at
their next bridge evening!

Tom is a complete all-rounder, a bit of a bounder!
If he was an alien, girls would want a close-
encounter!

And long after lunch, he's still out there!
He will continue, he'll not declare!
He has decided to just carry on
At least knock-up another tonne!
Demoralising the opposing team
With cover drives and reverse sweeps
His teammates hope to play, at some stage
But most of them don't even bother getting
changed!

Then Tom hears a whisper, and it puts him off!
And makes a dog's breakfast of his cut shot!
But he doesn't really seem to care!
As the ball fizzes off into the air
And one of the fielders makes an easy catch!
The crowd gasps among the cries of 'Owzat!'

Tom turns and grabs the umpire's waist!
Pulling him towards him into an embrace!
They start snogging in the middle of the field!
Their wandering hands now copping a feel!
Another loud gasp is heard from the crowd!
Sixteen ladies feint and hit the ground!

A woman chokes on her Victoria Sponge!
At the sight of these two men kissing with
tongues!
And as Tom pulls the umpire's trousers down
His teammates all rise with glee and shout
'He's out!! He's out!! He's out!!'

Go Large

When asked if I want large chips at the chippy
I should pause and proceed with caution!
Because instead of saying 'No, small please!'
I err on the size of portion!

2 X 2

Noah Smith knew that a flood was coming!
And he wanted to save God's creatures!
So he built a beautiful wooden ark
With lifeboats and other safety features

He knew he had to be very selective
Because he only had limited space
He'd only rescue two of each animal
As a few species were all he could save

He decided to take just famous animals
But he knew they'd be used to the best!
He invited them onto his luxury boat
That he hoped would impress the celebs!

Well, these star creatures were delighted!
Saying 'You've saved us, Noah, you hero!'
And they agreed to come straight away
Except Flipper, Moby Dick and Nemo!
(They weren't that bothered by the flood!)

Noah took his new friends in his SUV
From the city to the ark at the shore
Each pair of animals sat in the back
They came in 2x2 in his 4x4!

The giraffes stuck their heads through the sunroof
And the elephants were a bit of a squeeze!
The monkeys broke the windscreen wipers
While the picnic rug hid stowaway fleas

So, after many runs there and back
All the animals were finally boarded
The guests checked-in and went to their suites
And their passport details recorded

Nelly the Elephant unpacked her trunk
In a superior deluxe twin room
But she wasn't keen on sharing with Dumbo
In case he was planning on making a move!

Noah was only taking two birds of prey
Hedwig the Owl had been the first to arrive
The famous kestrel Kes stood in at the last minute
After the human, Eddie The Eagle, declined

The animals ordered oysters and champagne
All delivered to their luxury rooms
On Egyptian cotton, they lounged on huge beds
And were pampered by the ship's masseuse

Then, as expected, the heavens opened!
Torrential rain fell from the skies!
And it poured in biblical proportions!
For the next forty days and nights!

'I'm getting worried about all this rain!'
'If we start sinking, then I'm off!' said Roland Rat
'We don't care!' said the frogs, 'We'll find a lily pad!'
'Chill out!' said Sid the Sloth. 'Relax!'

As the ark floated off into the rising sea
The animals did 'relax' to relieve the tension!
Drinking one of the bars dry, in one single night!
And doing more lines than a schoolboy in detention!

Pepe Le Pew was told to leave the bar!
There'd been many complaints that he stunk!
He didn't care much cos he was so bladdered!
Yes, he WAS as drunk as a skunk!

So, the animals' gratitude and humility vanished
They started complaining and making demands!
Shouting 'Coming through! No autographs please!'
And 'Don't you know who I am?!'

Lassie and Shep were acting like they were entitled
And were behaving like a couple of divas!
Whilst Leo and Simba requested some strippers
So Noah sent them over some beavers!

Dolly the Sheep was bleating about the wifi
And all the cows were mooing about the grass
Dylan from *The Magic Roundabout* overheard
and said
'Grass? I can get you some of that!'

Many of the animals left the toilets in a mess
Miss Piggy and Porky Pig's room was a sty!
And Dumbo and Nelly snored like chainsaws
And kept half the ship awake every night!

As for the tigers, Tigger drove the waiters mad
Wanting free-flowing wine and raw meat!
And Tony wanted Frosties, as you'd expect
Because he thought 'they're grreat!' you see!

Paddington bought his own marmalade butties
Which he sneaked on-board in his case
But Pooh Bear wanted honey on his, so
He threw Paddington's sarnies away!

Mickey and Minnie wanted red carpet treatment
And a personal butler for their cabin!
They demanded either use of a huge waterbed
Or use of the Captains Quarters to shag in!

Bubbles the Chimp and Cheetah had egos
They thought they were the llama's pyjamas!

Swinging from the chandeliers, shouting rude
words
And raiding the kitchen for bananas!

Often, the animals were abusive to the staff!
Porky Pig told the captain to fuck himself!
The Cheshire Cat kept on smiling regardless
And on windows, Garfield stuck himself!

Dumbo wanted a tonne of sticky buns
But Nelly said 'No, you're getting fat!'
Dumbo got cross and stamped his feet
And part of the lower deck collapsed!

They had dinner, all together, every night
In the ship's long, grand, dining room
But they agreed not to eat each other
Cos that would just dampen the mood!

The animals kept on getting sloshed!
Shouting at the staff and barking orders!
Leo the Lion demanded dinner with the captain!
But he ran off and hid in his quarters!

Miss Piggy made a pig of herself, of course!
And she burped and her evening dress split!
Some say, she revealed herself on purpose!
And it was for Kermit The Frog's benefit!
When he saw her curvy porcine form

He had to go and cool down on the deck!
For his eyes boggled even more than usual
And went dizzy and had the frog sweats!

The rain stopped, and the floods subsided
After a long forty days and nights
Noah was exhausted and fed up with all
The constant greed, rudeness and gripes!

He concluded you could never meet
A more spoiled group of ungrateful animals!
Nearing Mount Ararat, where they'd dock next
day
He summoned them all to settle their bills!

And one by one, they refused saying 'No!'
'You should be paying *us! We're* the stars!'
'You should be honoured to have us on your boat!'
'Noah, don't you know who we are?!'

So, the animals would not back down
And Noah apologised despite his chagrin!
They demanded more oysters and champagne
And stormed back to their luxury cabins!

On the final night, they had a farewell dinner
And all got dressed up to the nines
But the giraffes needed help dressing
They couldn't reach to tie their bow ties!

They were seated in the great dining room
But soon they were starting to slouch!
They'd had an aperitif laced with Temazepam!
Which meant they were now *gouching out!*

They were getting sleepy, but were still hungry
Porky Pig drowsily moaned, 'Where's our food?!'
'Yeah, where's our food?!', slurred the animal
chorus
Noah said, 'The food is here! It's you!!'

They opened their eyes as Noah spoke again
'You're all spoilt and you'll get what you deserve!'
'Now, again, I've saved you ... for dinner!
'And tonight, we'll be happy to serve... *you!*'

Noah left as ten angry chefs entered
Wielding large, sharp cooking knives!
A coordinated attack from all angles
Took these defenceless animals' lives!

They cleaned and skinned each creature
And cut them into chunks and smaller bits
Then cooked the meat in enormous pots
On maximum heat - four hours, forty minutes
(Except the elephants – they take ten hours at
least!)

The staff were hungry when they eventually sat down
As the cooking had taken much time
But it was the most satisfying meal they'd ever had!
Because revenge was on the menu that night!

So, Lassie was made into a pasty!
And the horses were now main courses!
The dogs were prepared by the Korean chef
And what was in the *Katsu* curry? Can you guess?
And on the ark, *Tiger Barm* is a bread based dish!
It is not something soothing you put on your skin!
Oh, and Kermit's legs *do* taste like chicken!

So, if you'd like to book a table at The Ark Celebrity Animal Barbeque then ring 08915 22125842 and ask for Noah

Village Idiots

Our village is full of celebrities!
They've all come here to hide!
They've come to live in this bubble
To escape the harsh world outside!

Our barber is one Jeremy Paxman!
While cutting hair makes cutting remarks!
Many get up and tell Paxo to get stuffed
And shove his clippers right up his arse!

The vintner is Joseph Fritzel!
He sells many bottles of wine
He invited me down to his cellar
But I left and wisely declined!

Fred West lived in the town briefly
So most people kept their doors shut!
He tried to get a job as a bingo caller!
Whose numbers would've been up?!

That Katie Hopkins bought a house here
And the adjoining stables next door
And when hay was delivered to Katie's place
She was regularly mistaken for the horse!

Johnny Rotten rents a flat upstairs
But he's never there; it's pretty vacant!
Harold Shipman was the village doctor
But he was very short on patients!

The secondary school sacked its P.E. teacher
When they found out it was Gary Glitter!
And Hannibal Lecter has a butcher's shop
But I'm not really sure about the liver!

The scarecrow in the field is Jeremy Corben
Looking scruffy, dishevelled and tired
He was the perfect candidate though
No change of clothing was required!

James Corden, Simon Cowell and Piers Morgan
That's one monstrous celebrity trio!
And they all live in an enormous warehouse
It's the only place that can house their egos!

Our librarian was Brian Blessed
But it just didn't work out
Instead of whispering 'Shush!' he shouted
'GET THE FUCK OUT!"

So come and see our celebs, if you're ever passing
through
And just be grateful that they don't live near you!!

Fascist Dick Taylor

Hello! Good Morning, everybody!
Let me introduce myself to you!
My name is Richard Taylor, right now
But you'll be calling me 'Fuhrer' soon!

For I intend to take over this country!
Be the next leader of this land!
Then I'll expand further and beyond
Let me take you through my plans!

First, I'll declare my house as independent
It will be an autonomous state!
Secured by Big Derek and Psycho Steve
Who'll be guarding my garden gate!

And on top of my shed, I'm putting a podium
Made of mahogany and with my own crest!
Where I'll deliver rousing speeches to the
neighbours!
That'll get me noticed by the local press!

I'll need an army and then we can start
By ousting the government in a coup d'etat!
And forming a powerful military junta!
Recruiting soldiers from Wetherspoons punters!

How much to buy, bribe and get them on side?
I reckon a packet of crisps and a couple of pints!
Or maybe I'll introduce compulsory conscription!
They won't object, they've only *criminal*
convictions!

Fantasising about this war I've yet to start
I've been looking at tanks in *Exchange and Mart*
I want to award medals and all sorts of honours
Been looking on-line at short-range bombers!
I've even taken my daughter on fun trips
To see second-hand helicopter gunships!

For now, I'll run operations from my humble
abode
My bedroom's a good vantage point - I can see
down the road!
Later, I'll build a grand palace as my HQ
Cos there's nowt palatial about my terrace in
Goole!
I'll need somewhere befitting a mighty empire!
Where my subjects can come to stare and admire!
And in front, there'll be a giant marble statue of
me!
Eight hundred feet high, for everyone to see!

In a golden carriage, I'll be carried around
The masses will bow as I pass through the town!

I'll be saluted, admired, exalted and cheered
And idolised, worshipped, adored and revered!
The crowd will cry and greet me with awe!
Kim Jong Taylor is what I'll be called!

I think black and grey uniforms, what do you
think?
And sew on a scary logo to intimidate the public
Yes, we won't be wearing armbands at the pool!
Instead, we're going to wear them on our suits!
With a frightening image like a shark or a skull!
Coloured red! The same colour as... blood!

We'll take Huddersfield first, approach from the
south!
Then we'll march up the hill, straight into town!
Take control of Currys, Boots and Greggs!
And annex Argos, JD Sports and Next!
Then the town hall, police station and cinema too!
And we can feed popcorn and pick and mix to all
the troops!

We'll get all the armed forces on our side!
Through every town, we'll march with pride!
And county by county, we will prevail!
We will be victorious; we will not fail!
We'll be in Number Ten in a matter of weeks!
And bring the Prime Minister to his knees!
Then the rest of the world will soon be ours!

Until we're the only global superpower!
And if any country puts up any resistance!
We'll bomb the bastards out of existence!

But once the world's ours, we can move on at
pace!
The moon and the near planets as we conquer
space!
I'll move off-world to run operations from afar!
Maybe I can build my own Death Star?!

So, join me Ladies and Gentlemen, sign up here!
Let's take over this world and rule by fear!
We'll start by taking over this great nation!
Take part in this wonderful self-invasion!

What if it all goes wrong you wonder?
We can go and hide in my coal bunker!
There's another question you all want to ask?
No, Ladies and Gentlemen, I am definitely NOT
mad!!

Meep! Meep!

A.M.

I'm crouched in Pearl Harbour behind a wall
With Lord Byron, Brian Cant and Eric Hall
When bombs start falling all around
Me and Kate Winslet hit the ground
As bullets whizz over our heads
I tell her I've got a new waterbed
Beep, Beep, Beep! That's a funny air-raid siren!
Kate grows frog's legs and hops off with Byron
Then brightness as it all fades away
Rousing, eyelids open, awake!

Beep, Beep, Beep!
Reality hits, I'm no longer asleep
Bang down the button that says 'Off'
On that noisy, bastard alarm clock!

Lips stuck to teeth
This Humfrey Bogart
Pulls back the sheets
Releasing an old fart
Also known as me!

Eyes edged with sleep dust and gunk
Half-closed, part-cemented shut
Looks of a wet weekend in Cleethorpes
Breath of a freshly excavated corpse

Hair - Ken Dodd, voice - Barry White
Comatose, now vertical, stumble for a shite
I'm touching cloth, I head for the bog
With all the speed of a tranquilised sloth

I have the odour of a tramp's caravan
My face? Reversed over by a bread van
My throat dryer than the Atacama
Lumber downstairs now still in pyjamas
I flop down onto the leather sofa
Feels like I've not slept since last October

I can only grunt before half past ten
I'm nocturnal, I don't do 'A.M.'
So come back another time
I'm just too tired to... rhyme!

I just can't speak
Until I've had my coffee!
So don't talk to me!
I'm going...
Fuckoffee!

A Day at the Races

Two pally couples are off to the races!
Dean and Wendy with Wayne and Stacey
Joining other racegoers in a lairy horde
A giant mob descending on the racecourse

Stacey has bought a new dress for her 'fun day'
She's left the tags on; she's returning it on
Monday!
She'll bleach the Sambuca stains, Febreze the
armpits
And Sellotape the back after the inevitable arse
split!

And Wendy sees herself as pretty regal
But she's got the manners of a Newquay Seagull!
Cos she's really just a Council Estate Barbie!
The nearest she'll get to royalty is *Doing Charlie!*

To create the facade of looking smart and minted
The girls buy fascinators on eBay or Vinted
The boys in suits from a Next clothing clearance
Worn only once, for their last court appearance

There are few more loathsome men than Dean
and Wayne!
But their overtime brings in a reasonable wage

Which their wives spaff in spas or naff boutiques
Glad their odious men work six days a week!

First, to the *Slag and Lettuce* for a 'cheeky' pint
Which quickly turns to three, four and five
Then stagger down to the racecourse gates
To queue with the other inebriated apes
Past cops with poorly trained sniffer dogs
And now they're in, a hunt for the bogs!
But there's a queue for the Armitage Shanks
So everyone pisses behind the burger van!

Such an elegant occasion this will be!
Packed into the enclosure like sardines
Racegoers pushing and jostling at the bar
Desperate for the racing and drinking to start

And two hours later, the meet's in full swing
A few races have run but nobody's watching
Stacey has fallen over, passed out on the floor!
Skirt up, legs akimbo, like a fifty-pence whore!

What a high-class event the races are today!
Foul-mouthed women partnering tanked-up apes
Bottles in hands, staggering through the stands
Arrested after vomiting in a policeman's hat!

It's not long before the first punch is thrown!
As it all kicks-off in this hellish war zone!

Each blow is followed by a headbutt chaser!
It's like Gaza here but there's a bit safer!

A steaming Dean says, 'Me horse didn't come in!'
Before lamping the guy sat next to him!
As Wayne sells some drugs outside the loos!
To the mounted policemen and the stewards too!

In between the usual fighting and marauding
The men are downing pints and applauding
The girls flash at any photographer with a Nikon!
Then onto a blanket they haven't yet been sick on!

Wendy bins her hat slurring 'Fuck the dress code!'
Half-remembering she left her knickers at home!
Holding onto strangers as Lambrini is necked
Not noticing she's shat down the back of her leg!

Cleaning-up next day is an army of staff
Removing litter, vomit and broken glass
The locals that have been under siege
Trapped in their homes can finally leave
But next month, there's another race!
Another day of booze and hate!
Of betting slips and busted lips
Half-eaten burgers and the waft of piss
Discarded condoms and snapped chip forks
Just another morning after the night before!
Down at the damned, bloody racecourse!

U Bend, The Rules

(To display on the back of toilet doors at work)

We request when using this toilet
That you don't soil or spoil it
Unless you want to get bollocked!
Please don't spray and splatter
Your horrible faecal matter
We don't want a Jackson Pollock!

And please, please don't wee
On the floor and on the seat!
We don't want to use
Half a litre of *Flash*
To clean up your slash!
Please respect the loo!

If your shite, the walls are adorning
You might get a verbal warning!
Because HR knows *everything!*
They *log* all of your ablutions
Toilet noises and air-pollution
With hidden devices under the rim!

And don't get too flushed
If the stench is too much
Hold your nose and don't breathe!
And if there's no toilet roll
Just use your own clothes
Wipe your arse with your sleeve!

Thank you,
The Cleaner x

Snowman and Wife

He stands and he just stares
Under that top hat he wears
Through our window he gazes
I glare back at him for ages
But still he doesn't flinch
Neither of us move an inch

I wonder if he's actually cold?
And where does he get his clothes?
Oh, and is that red scarf of his
One of mine he's nicked? Or a gift?

But something feels awry!
It's all down to my wife!
That cold pillock's on her mind!
She talks about him all the time!

She's out, every day, to pat his chest and arse!
And comes back to tell me, that he's still rock
hard!
Oh, and she's carved him a six-pack with a trowel!
And she calls him the *Abdominal* Snowman now!

If, like the blackbirds, she's given him a peck
I'll take his scarf and wrap my hands around his
bloody neck!

173

And I swear he smiles when she's out in the garden
And even worse than that, I sure his carrot hardens!
Does he watch her getting changed?
Has he had his cold, wicked way?
Has she fallen for his icy charms?
And into his... sticks-for-arms?

Has that slut undone his coal buttons?
Has she been on her knees sucking on a Mr Freeze?

I accused her of seeing that snowy twat!
She denied it and said I'm just being daft!
Then I came home from work and called her a whore!
When I found icy footprints on the bedroom floor!
And it was frosty in there, but then, what's new?!
Had she had, what they call in DIY, *a frozen screw*?!

And I've jammed on the heating!
So he can't come inside the house... Or her!

And I'm not waiting for the thaw
Or for a slightly warmer spell
He's for the slaughter!
He's going back to water!
He's gonna melt in fiery hell!

She might carry a torch for him
But I'll carry one too, I'll join in!
My *blow* torch, that's what I need!
Now where's my extension lead?!

Personal Trainer

If she quit, I wouldn't blame her!
It's a challenge being my personal trainer!
She's ex-marines, so it doesn't faze her!
She's determined to shape this flabby waster!

Her name is Joanne Starling
Or, as I call her, *Jo Stalin!*
She trains her clients hard, she's very demanding!
Her sessions feel a bit like the Normandy
Landings!

I remember the day that I called her
It must have been in a fit of pique!
After some kids had shouted 'FB!' at me
And they didn't mean Facebook, I think!

I recall when we had our first session
She came over and shook my hand
My wrist felt like it'd been crushed by an
anaconda!
Then driven over by a delivery van!

She said she could lift me over her head!
I said 'Your free to give it a try!'
She looked me up and down, then backed out
And said 'I don't fancy being paralysed!'

She threw me straight on the bloody bike!
And said 'Let's see how fit you are!'
She weighed me and recorded my height
And painfully pinched the fat on my arms!

'You should be measured on a weighbridge!', she said
'Do you know, you're much too heavy?!'
'Have protein shakes, exercise, lift weights!'
I said 'The only thing I lift, are bevvies!'

She said 'Sit-ups, now! Lie down!'
'And put that bloody pie down!'
'Come on, don't let the side down!'
I thought, 'I wish you'd pipe down!'

She said, 'Don't drink beer, drink water!'
And talked about the importance of hydration
And that I should get a good night's sleep
Not sat all night watching *Babestation!*

She wanted to see 'a vast improvement'!
And wobbled my belly, saying it was just like jelly!
Then asked me to do something called 'movement'!
Said documentaries about people like me are on the telly!

She wanted me to give one hundred percent!
Something I'd never done before!
I said, 'I doubt I'll get anywhere near that!'
'Percentage wise, I give about four!'

She wouldn't let me wear my jeans in the gym!
And made me wear shorts and a vest!
She wanted me to heave and strain!
And get covered in something called 'sweat'!

She put me on a rower then a treadmill!
Basically, she put me through the wringer!
Told me to eat oats for breakfast, fish for lunch
And other boring and dull things for dinner!

I told her what I ate for the previous day
So she hauled me over the coals!
Then emptied my pockets as her trained sniffer
dog
Checked my gym bag for sausage rolls!

But I had the last laugh because
I had half a Bounty hidden in each shoe!
She asked me why I was limping but
I told her it was an old war wound!

She went on about my weight and diet
And I needed to watch my blood pressure!

And had I thought about meditation?
And less stress! But *she* was the stressor!

And once, she had a right go at me!
She said she drove past and saw me in KFC!
I said there's no way that could possibly be!
Cos I was in McDonald's that day you see!

And now? Am I a lean, mean machine?

I'm a lost cause, there's no point at all!
I cannot even lift a medicine ball!
And as a trainer, I'd wouldn't rate her!
Cos I'm *still* not arsed, I'm *Mr UnMotivator!*

Now, Jo's looking for me everywhere around the town!
Cos I've avoided training for six months now!
She posted some threats through my door!
If I don't come to the gym, she'll remove my balls!

So, I am going into hiding for a few weeks!
In the cellar at a friend's, if anyone wants me
If you see her, and she asks where I am
Tell her I have moved to Suriname!

Chickenshit

Scott! You've been sussed! The truth is out!
You've been shouting your mouth off around the town!
Telling anyone you can find who'll listen
About your military experience and dangerous missions!

The story that you've been trying to pedal
Is you fought in a war and got awarded medals!
And your platoon was captured behind enemy lines!
Which you single-handedly rescued and got home alive!

You did many tours and fought several wars!
According to your counterfeit military record!
It's just a big pack of lies, deceit and fakery!
You spent that time in Bury, working in a bakery!

You said you saw action in Afghanistan!
But really, you lived in Acton, in the back of a van!
And we know you didn't serve in the Falklands!
You really served in a caff called *Folk Land!*

You purchased war militaria to spin your yarn!
And needed a uniform to help look the part!
You thought a *get-up* would impress the ladies!
So bought combat gear from the *Army and Navy!*

But it turns out, you're a spineless fellow!
You are every single shade of yellow!
The colour of the Sun and the colour of mustard!
You are a real cowardly custard!

You're scared of spiders, rats, cats and dogs!
Paper clips, zips, balloons and frogs!
You sleep with the light on cos you're afraid of the dark!
Night manoeuvres in Kosovo? You're talking through your arse!

You're terrified of buttons, heights and tight spaces!
Crowds, water and red shoelaces!
Nearly every sort of phobia that exists!
I'd write them all down but you're afraid of lists!

You're a lying, fibbing, shaky kneed weed!
You're a mythomaniac, Jeffrey Archer in fatigues!
You're a bullshitter, Pinocchio, a porky teller!
You're Bill Clinton or that Boris Johnson fellah!

You say you've the courage of a lion!
Tell all that you have no fear!
But if you were a tank in a war
You'd only have a reverse gear!

You spend most of your time
Stood quaking in your boots!
They say you're afraid of ducks!
And wouldn't say boo to a goose!

You're a yellow belly, quivering like a jelly!
Hiding behind the sofa when Dr Who is on the telly!

You're a real scaredy cat!
But, in fact, you're a chicken too!
If we were in France, if I had the chance
I say to you, 'Poulet Vous!'

Some local squaddies haven't taken too kindly
To you pretending to be one of them!
Their gonna strip you, paint your bottom blue!
And tattoo 'Fake War Hero' on your head!

Some other guys are planning to end your life
But nobody will give a damn, I'm afraid!
You'll be buried with no military honours just
'FOR STOLEN VALOUR' on the headstone of your grave!

The Death of a Traffic Warden

Oh, hello there, Officer!
What brings you to my door?!
The village traffic warden's been murdered?!
Gosh! Did I see anything? No, nothing at all!

Do I know anyone who'd do him harm?
Well, how long have you got?!
It's not a secret, if I'm honest that
He wasn't popular in these parts!

He, for certain, was not a people person!
He got grief but gave so much ammunition!
He inspired hate, he was a snake on the take!
On a mission for commission with no contrition!

He never saw anybody else's point of view!
He never gave the benefit of the doubt!
He couldn't see sense, only pound signs!
All he wanted to do was to write tickets out!

When he arrived, he was received with open arms
Because we're quite a hospitable bunch!
But soon, he was as welcome as a fart in a
spacesuit!
Or a bagel at a Labour party lunch!

See, our village traffic warden could not be trusted
He'd give you a ticket even when rules were
obeyed!
He would creep about to catch people out
And got ten percent of every fine that was paid!

I heard that he would take bribes sometimes!
If he nicked you and you offered him a tenner
He wouldn't write you a ticket, say he'd let you off
But you'd get one in the post a week later!

Officer, there are so many suspects
You could fill a whole A4 pad!
He has angered pretty much everyone!
Made so many people hopping mad!

There's Steve on the market who sells fruit and
veg
And there's Jane who runs the corner shop
Steve said he'd love to go and boil his head
And Jane wants to slice off his cock!

There's *Mad Maisie*, she's the Librarian
She's a little bit odd, somewhat kooky
I heard she saved up for an assassin!
Or maybe it was just a Suzuki?!
Officer, my hearing is not what it was...

Ken's the village butcher and a karate instructor!
He wanted to give him the chop!
And Sue, the lollipop lady, said if
He *did* have a heart, she hoped it'd... STOP!
I overheard some guys in the pub say
They wanted to go out and leather him!
They said he would pay in a medieval way!
And planned to tar and feather him!

In that damned uniform he would strut
Who the hell did he think he was?!
He saw himself as a little kerbside Hitler!
Or a sort of five-foot-five parking god!

Who'd want to kill such a *dedicated* worker?
Hiding behind the bushes, lying in wait
Hunkered down, concealed in an unmarked van
Nicking a disabled woman returning a minute
late!

Oh, course I am a bit indifferent really
As I never actually met the chap
But I sympathise with the anger of people
Who had been targeted by this evil twat!

He would always say to his victims
That he was only enforcing the law
But then, why did the entire village want
To slam his head in a fucking car door?!

Am I getting upset? Yes, a bit!
What was that film he was in?
Crouching Bastard, Hidden Prick!

'Got you! You are sixty seconds late!'
Well, now it's *him* who is late!
Apologies Officer, that was in poor taste!

Where was *I* you'd like to know?
Well, I have an alibi, I was at home!
No! I was playing cards at the Monday club!
It was a Tuesday, you say? Fuck!
Oh sorry, I remember I was watching TV
The jumper and beard - Noel Edmonds, I think?
He's not on TV anymore? Ah, probably a repeat!
On that channel - it's called *Dave* or is it *Pete*?

He said he got no commission; he lied to us!
Said that he never, ever got a cut!
Well, he's had one *now!* About twenty!
That detail was never released?!
You misheard me, I said 'plenty!'
Anyway, that guy was a waste of life!
I suppose he deserved to have been knifed!
You didn't tell me he was stabbed?!
Hang on, this is making me look bad!

Anyway, I was busy at 9.35pm on the 3rd!
You didn't tell me when the incident occurred?!

Just a lucky guess, I suppose!
And who'd dump him in a bin behind Tesco?!
How did I know?!
You'll have to excuse me. I've got to go!

Yeah, don't worry, I'm not going far!
I've just got to go and move my car!
I had nowhere to park last night, I was late home!
So I had to park on some double yellows!

Mind you, I've no need to worry about that now....

She's Not Great

She's not great!
She never gives and always takes!
Tried to cut the cables on my brakes!
She's not great!

She's not fantastic!
Her knickers have no elastic!
She once shat in a wicker basket!
She's not fantastic!

She's got no charm!
She's got track marks on her arms!
Knows how to disable a burglar alarm!
She's got no charm!

She's not a catch!
Got the morals of an alley cat!
Smells like the shell of a hermit crab!
She's not a catch!

She's not neat!
She's mouthy and indiscreet!
Her labia look like doner meat!
She's not neat!

But of course, though, I'll have to concede
She's way, way, way out of my league!

The Third Person

I'm sorry I slept with your twin sister - I thought it
was you!
I did comment at the time
When I was doing her from behind
'Where's that mole on your back gone to?'

Zen and the Art of Skilful Avoidance

In life, we meet people we love, like and respect
And those we loathe or that bore or annoy
These folks, we don't want contact with
And we'll do anything to try and avoid!

Well, true enlightenment is here my friends!
You can dodge those you've shunned or spurned!
Come and learn *The Art of Skilful Avoidance!*
And don't jump all the bridges you've burned!

Whether you are trying to evade exes or their
parents
Former mates, friends of friends or just relatives
Or old bosses, teachers or classmates from school
Or just boring people, you know, *human
sedatives!*

If you're dodgy, do you want to avoid the police?
Or those you owe money to, or once flashed at?
Boasty old school mates doing better than you
now
Or one-night stands you had and never rang back!

When you enter a supermarket, don't walk too
fast!

You may find you'll have to duck for cover!
A mountain of baked beans or large cereal display
Means you can hide from that angry ex-lover!

When having a little mooch around the store
Always peep around the corner of each aisle!
And when you've checked that the coast is clear
You can proceed using caution and guile!

If there's nobody there that boils your piss
Or wishes to play football with your head!
Move stealthily, eyes open, around the store
Or go home, shop on-line instead!

Use a small trolley, they're more manoeuvrable
Say, if your nemesis is in the frozen food section
You can turn on your heels, do an *about turn*
And whizz off in the opposite direction!

If need be, dump your basket on the floor
And walk quickly right out of the shop!
Don't look suspicious, like you've stolen
something!
Look like your guts are about to drop!

At the theatre, check the stalls and the circle
And when stood at the bar, keep watch!
If in trouble, hide behind the stage curtain
Or the cardboard cut-out of Joe Swash!

In the chippy, is your ex in the queue for food?
Cos if they dumped you because of your weight
And you're ordering a large pasty and chips
Then you're bang to rights (with a pie), I'm afraid!

In the pub, just go in and scan the tables
If there's someone you don't want to see
Talk on your phone and walk straight out
Like you've somewhere important to be!

If you are ambling down the street and
Your old boss passes that you want dead!
Resist the urge to punch their lights out!
Put your hood up; cross the road instead!

If the object of your desire walks towards you
And you're scruffy, a mess and just rained on!
Dodge into the nearest shop you can find
Even Ann Summers with a dildo sale on!

Ladies, if you've spotted your ex on a train
Sat three rows behind with some bimbo!
Get up quietly and hide in the bog
Or throw yourself out of the window!

In the park, if you see someone annoying
You can hide behind a bush or a tree
Or just roll around on the ground
Completely cover yourself in leaves!

When filling up with fuel at the petrol station
And there's a big bloke you've pissed off!
Pay at the pump then quickly drive away
Like you're leaving a Formula 1 pit stop!

And if someone moves into a house near you
A prick that you just cannot abide!
Sooner or later, you'll bump into them
Sometimes, there's really nowhere to hide!

Grow a beard or wear shades and a hat
Have plastic surgery to disguise your face!
Then move away, preferably abroad
And get a restraining order, just in case!

Oh, hello Richard! Richard Ware?
I didn't see you standing there!
Blimey! I've not seen you for years!
You used to call me 'Four Eyes' and 'Big Ears'!
I've not seen you since school!
What have you been up to?
You run your own successful Management
Consultancy?
What about me?
Am I free for a catch-up?
Fuck!

Posh

Good evening, old chap!
It's quiet in here tonight!
I don't think we've met before?
My name is Hugo Wright

Do you mind if I ask you something?
Perhaps you could put me straight?
I don't think you are from these parts?
Clothes and shoes giveth a man away!

I do hope that you're not lost?
Or maybe feeling out of place?
The great and the good drink in here
We're the masters of our race!

Perhaps you're a little shell-shocked?
By the prices of these drinks?
Or how we dress or our wealth?
Did you take a wrong turn, do you think?

Sit, join me for a minute, old chap!
And take in this fine interior!
Look, I've ordered us a whiskey, relax!
And I'll tell you why I'm superior!

I'm going to make some assumptions
Or should that be some presumptions?
You see...

You and I are from different stock!
I am posh and you are not!
Some people *just have* breeding!
While some people *are just* breeding!

I have designs on a yacht and an expensive watch!
You've holes in your socks and a wee-stained
crotch!

I have a larder in my kitchen!
You have a Lada in your garage!
I buy fine art with my money!
You have a poster of Nigel Farage!

I live on a country estate
Where I often go shooting!
You live on a council estate
Where you often go shooting!

I drive a big posh Audi!
You buy your nosh at Aldi!
I am Aga!
You are Argos!

I am Dunhill!
You are dunghill!
I buy my stereos from B & O!
You buy your Oreos from B & M!

I am new Maserati!
You are old Mazda!
I am black tie at the BAFTAs!
You are black tea from ASDA!
I am posh!
You are not!

I am haute cuisine!
Ha! I don't mean *oat* cuisine!
What do I mean?
Porridge, man!
I suppose *you're* more egg, chips and beans!

I am Upper Class, you're on your uppers!
I am Beluga caviar, you are fish suppers!

I say, 'What what?!'
You say, 'You wot?!'

So, as I'm much better than you
I will now say 'toodle-oo'!
Oh, it's time to pay?!
My wallet seems to have been mislaid!
You couldn't lend me tenner, could you?

Miss Treat

She pats me hard on top of my head!
Makes me kip on the end of the bed!
I curl up and try to get some sleep
While my girlfriend's engrossed in trash TV

She doesn't like animals, she never has!
Or humans either, as a matter of fact!
But mainly it is cats that she dislikes
Says they have pointy ears and evil eyes!

And she insists I am like a chubby cat!
Lazy, hairy, greedy and fat!
And while that's a fair description of me
I'll take being compared to a cute moggy!

Well maybe, I should scratch her face!
That would put her in her place!
And even if I *did* have nine lives
They'd all be miserable by *her* side!

She often moves me off my seat!
I really haven't landed on my feet!
I am, *apparently*, under hers!
If I *was* a cat, I'd never purr!

She never picks me up, only puts me down!
Says when I'm hungry, I follow her around!
If I *was* her pet, she'd take me to the vet!
And she'd get me 'done', you can bet!

On the garden roses, she makes me poop!
Feeds me in a bowl, OK, so it's soup!
For a fishy treat, she makes me beg!
Pushes my head between her legs!

But one day, I finally cracked!
I just had to get my own back!
While she was putting on her glad rags
I curled a turd in her handbag!

And when she returned home, we had a fight!
Cos the contents of her bag was covered in shite!
And she just threw me out into the night
But I went to a club and had the time of my life!

I mated with a *Cat,* I think she was on heat!
Well, she was *in season* if you know what I mean!
Katrina was her name
And like the storm...
She blew me like a hurricane!

Santa Banter

Please Santa!
Forgive me!
It was just banter!

I'm sorry for acting like a prick last night!
For the opprobrium and invective, I apologise!
Unfortunately, in your direction, words were spat
I called you a tosspot and a fat, bearded twat!

I had a few too many, I'll admit!
I was a bit vile and mean-spirited
I'm regretful for my vitriol and my spite
I blame it on the bottles of Lapland wine!

I didn't really mean what I said
That I'd like to see you drop dead!
I didn't mean to be so unkind
Saying Mrs Claus must be blind!

Can I respectfully state
That I didn't mean to say
That you should go fuck yourself
And that you fuck your elves!

I said Cupid should be killed by an arrow; that's
bad!
And Donner should be turned into a meaty kebab!
And Prancer should just leap off a cliff!
And Blitzen put in a blender and blitzed!

I know it doesn't make it right!
It seemed funny in the pub at the time!
But now, I'm paying the price for what I said
Feels like a rhino is tap dancing on my head!

I didn't mean to intimate
That you had been intimate!
With your elven helpers!
In your cosy tax shelter!
And regret that I said
The one colour that doesn't suit you is... red!

That Mrs Claus is a cheap, old whore!
And she's usually knickerless, Saint Nicholas!

I regretfully said these things and I quote:
'You're a washed up old alkie in a furry coat!'
'You're a lazy git, working one day a year!'
'The rest of the time on the booze and the gear!'
And I said the elves play with your bulging sack!
But please forgive me, I take it all back!

I've had a bone to pick with you since I was eight!
You came down our chimney in a drunken state!
Instead of leaving us lots of great pressies
You knocked over the tree and stole the telly!

You only visit good children but it's ironic you see
Cos I have evidence of *you* being *very* naughty!
You took those stable boys back to your grotto!
And you all did some coke and got quite blotto!
It turned into something incredibly sordid!
It became Lapland's biggest ever orgy!
Santa, I'm not saying that you're secretly gay
But you were *behind* those boys *all the way!*
The video was recorded on somebody's phone
Which I now have, you'll be sorry to know!
And there's other photos taken of you, without
permission!
Of you and the reindeers in a compromising
position!

I do apologise to you and your wife, profusely
And this Christmas, please don't refuse me!
I'll leave you a mince pie and a glass of sherry
If you furnish me with a couple of pressies
A Rolex and a Ferrari would be gratefully
received!
And those negatives will be burned immediately!
So, Merry Christmas to you, Mr Claus!
You perverted, drunken, sad, old bore!

Lightning Rod

In a double-quick time, he explodes like
dynamite!
Called by bored ladies, he's their dial-a-ride!

Cos Rodney Jones lives his life to the fullest!
Has sex faster than a speeding bullet!

See him go and see him come!
Two minutes flat and he is done!

He's like greased lightning, so quick it's
frightening!
He's soon done the job with his fleshy piping!

He's been and gone, done the deed!
It's not long before he's sown his seed!

He's straight in and then straight out!
He doesn't like to hang about!

A quick joyride doesn't take much time!
Leaves the engine running on his scooter outside!

Girls, there's barely time to kiss him!
If you blink, your bound to miss him!

Foreplay isn't something he need consider!
He comes after work but he's home for dinner!

Sometimes he doesn't even remove his coat!
Gives instant porridge when he gets his oats!

Because he's the fastest draw in the West!
You can use him to time a boiled egg!

But some of his ladies decided to revolt!
Started calling him Usain 'Shot His' Bolt!
And they felt unsatisfied and short-changed
Upset that it was always only *him* that came!
So, they rang up his best friend instead
Who properly undressed and got into bed
He'd make them moan, scream and writhe
And he could do it multiple times!
A quick reloader and a stayer, not a leaver!
Now the one they call is... *Peter the Repeater*!

I Wanna Be A Train Driver

I want a job that's not much mither!
That doesn't make me a skiver!
Cos I don't wanna be a high flyer!
Or a corporate ladder climber!
I just want to be a train driver!

I want something that's not too taxing!
With very little moving or reacting!
Don't want anything that's exacting!
A job that's heavy on relaxing!

In the cab, king of my castle!
And without that thing called 'hassle'!
One hand on the *dead man's handle*
Tossing off, flicking through *Razzle!*

I want the uniform and the hat!
And a train driver's leather bag!
And a stroke of the stations' cat!
And shag dirty women in my cab!

Take bags of pies to feed my gut!
Press two buttons and read *The Sun!*
Chill, until the working day is done!
And get paid far, far, far too much!

Unions will say I'm within my rights
To turn up late or when I like!
But my dream is to go out on strike!
'Commuters! Get on your bikes or take a hike!'
'*I* won't be taking you passengers for a ride!'

I'll apply to be a train driver, straightaway!
I fancy a Porsche when I get my first wage!
I won't even really need to use my brain!
Just think, one day, I'll be driving *your* train!

Monster Mensch

A hopeless, decrepit, Northern town
Where nothing good is going down
Some say this place feels like it's cursed
Cos every day feels like October 31st!

Truanting from poor-performing schools
Forms of girls form gangs of ghouls
Shuffling into flaking shops of decay
Painted faces hide the sallow and grey
Through vacant stores, with vacant stares
Stolen roll-on and concealed concealer stashed for
their lairs!

And zombie boys lumber down the aisles
All modelling their *JD Sports Direct* styles
Whilst saloned, taloned, nagging vampires
Flick through the *Argos Catalogue* of their desires
Dragged their blokes away from sport on the telly
Men who would have inspired Mary Shelley!

The employment dreams of a youth disaffected
Lie in a retail park that has never been erected
Twenty years of plans but not one brick has been
laid!
The inertia of council planners living thirty miles
away

Looking like the product of a lab experiment
They steal for cash and their own merriment
They speak a tongue but not like ours!
And they seek to take and to devour!
No point reporting a crime around here!
Necrotic pickpockets thieve without fear
Another bike stolen by the leisure centre
The police won't say, 'We'll catch you later!'

When the sun goes down, there's not much change
Because the town is shadowed by black and grey
Only coloured by pavement pizza or puddles of blood
Spilt last night outside the Working Men's Club!

Lycanthrope blokes stagger from ASDA now
Swigging cheap beer as they head into town
Red-eyed, their sharp fizzogs crumpled and ugly
Cauliflowered like they've played years of rugby
Malodorous, becapped, unkempt and hairy
Tattooed, snarling, malevolent and scary
In naff gold chains but *out* on bail
In a pub with more criminals than a jail!

Black sportswear shrouds under-age teens
These ravens skulk by the fruit machines
And the older Romeos are such catches!
Asking girls to show their boobs and snatches

Scowling scarlet faces, showing their hardness
Every single one, a Prince of Darkness!
Or out wearing their congenital horror masks
Padded coats cloak blades or baseball bats
Those bats don't fly like the Spice will tonight!
Profitably dealing on the bikes they bestride

There'll be no daylight here, anytime soon!
Every night in the sky, there's a Full Moon!
But, of course, it's not actually Halloween
Or a terrifying dream; it's reality!
So, ask yourself:
Are you brave enough to venture
Into ███ town centre?!

(Insert your nearest shithole in the blank above)

Which Doctor?

My local GP surgery
Is getting far too big!
There's now so many doctors!
Do you want to hear the list?
OK then, there's...

Doctor Small
Doctor Large
Doctor Blunt
Doctor Sharp

Doctor House
Doctor Street
Doctor Robert
Doctor Beat

Doctor Crippen
Doctor Phibes
Doctor Morecambe
Doctor Wise

Doctor Evil
Doctor Good
Doctor Robin
Doctor Hood

Doc Martin
Doctor Phil
Doctor Jack
Doctor Jill

Doctor Hale
Doctor Pace
Doctor Will
Doctor Grace

Doctor Burns
Doctor Wood
Doctor Waters
Doctor Brook

Doctor Singh
Doctor Song
Doctor Wright
Doctor Wong

Doctor Black
Doctor White
Doctor Jekyll
Not Mr Hyde!

Doctor Ware
Doctor Watt
Doctor Who
Doctor Spock

Doctor Love
Doctor Hook
Doctor Page
Doctor Book

Doctor Hart
Doctor Head
Doctor Hope
And Doctor Dread

I use this rhyme to recall all the GPs
Cos remembering them is a bit of a chore!
But you think you're gonna see a doctor?
There's more chance of seeing a unicorn!

Meat and Potato Pilot

They call Dan 'The Meat and Potato Pilot'!
As he's been having far too much to eat!
And now, the co-pilot has to sit by the toilets!
Cos in the cockpit, Dan takes up both seats!

The airline said, 'Dan, lose weight quickly!'
'This is a warning! You have been told!'
'The cockpit can't cope with the strain now!'
'The only place you can sit is the hold!'

So, Dan when up to Scotland for a while
Where he let nothing but salad pass his lips!
But when he got back, he'd gained three stone!
Cos Scottish salads are doner meat and chips!

In the end, the airline sacked him!
But he did not give one single shit!
He went to America and got a job straight away!
Because to the Yanks, he was anorexic!

Me and the Bearded Ladies

We went shopping yesterday to Sainsbury's
I took myself and The Bearded Ladies
But people were cruel, on their worst behaviour!
They kept pointing to the aisle that sells the
razors!

I think those folks just wanted to hurt us!
They're jealous of girls who work at the circus!
Or envious of the unusual look they have!
W.G. Grace or Brian Blessed in drag!

You may wonder why I wanted to pursue
Girls like them who are so very hirsute?
Well, I'll go out with a hairy lady, if I want to!
Cos their beards give me something to hang onto!

Clothes Don't Suit

Most clothes don't suit me
And suits make me look fat!
Gloves make me look stupid
And I look a twat in a hat!

And a turd in a shirt!
An oaf in a coat!
A fool in shoes!
An arse with a scarf!
A dork in shorts!
An anus in trainers!
A dong in a sarong!
A tool in a cagoule!
A molester in a sou'wester!
And a goon in pantaloons!

I look a right vagina, in chav or designer!

A zombie in Abercrombie!
An ass in Adidas!
A weasel in Diesel!
A burke in Burberry!
A dunghill in Dunhill!
And a tit in Paul Smith!

I look in the wardrobe in despair!
There's really nowt that I can wear!
So, I'm binning all my clothes soonest!
And I'm going to become a nudist!

That's put you off your dinner, hasn't it?!

The Kit Kat Man

Don't shake hands
With the Kit Kat Man!

Chocolate digits behind his back
You can smell him from afar!
For this scruffy old tramp
Sticks his fingers up his arse!

He'll offer you his hand
But refuse and walk away!
Unless you want your mitts
Stained a different shade!

His grubby, old beige coat
Is caked in brown flecks!
And he's always fiddling
Down the back of his keks!

Don't shake hands
With the Kit Kat Man!

His fingers are excremental!
He scratches and scrapes!
Deep up into his anus!
They dig and excavate!

Constipated, dehydrated
His turds are profoundly stuck!
Halfway in, halfway out
His stool, he's trying to pluck!

Don't think twice! You'll pay the price!
If you don't follow this sage advice!
If you don't want your hands
Immediately tanned!
Please don't shake hands
With the Kit Kat Man!

People Are Like Fruit

Do you think people are like fruit?
Well, some of them actually are!
Graham Norton, Elton John
And Alan Carr!

Let's test the theory on my friends!

There's Tony, he's like a strawberry
Seedy, with a fragrant scent!
Barry is like a banana
Comes in boxes and he's bent!

Sheila is like a grape
She is easily made to wine!
Small, thin skinned but
Moist and tastes divine!

Bob is like a pineapple
Big and quite prickly!
Dean is like a durian fruit
Rough looking and sickly!

Dan is a bad apple
Rotten to the core!
But Laura is a Kiwi
Eaten *down under* in the raw!

Linda is like a satsuma
Juicy and easily peeled!
Amy is freshy dug rhubarb
Tart and dirty in a field!

So, I have these mates, I am lucky indeed!
Friends like these don't grow on trees!
Er... hang on!

Civil Phwoah

If a woman or man, you physically admire
Happens to pass your way
Shouldn't you be able to let them know?
To say, just *respectfully* state
That you are a fan of their form?
Use a non-threatening call?
Let's call it a *Civil Phwoah*!

In these days of Wokeism and PC
We all have to tread more carefully!
Maybe we can show desire without taking risks?
Nothing sexist, misogynistic or misandrist
A hushed comment; polite, quiet clamour
Not in a pushy or aggressive manner!

But how to word it without sounding too
offensive?
So as not to make someone go on the defensive?
Well, try to not alarm the person in question
By alerting them gently to your intentions

Maybe this?:

'Can I say, in quiet, soft tones?'
'That I'd like to jump your bones!'

Or:

'Can I state, if you please don't mind?'
'I'd like to do you rigid from behind!'

Or:

'Can I mention, if you've no objection?'
'That you've given me a massive extension!'

Ladies! Don't shout things like:
'I'm the Sex Express! Come, climb aboard!'
Gentlemen! Please don't say:
'Here! Grab my sword! It's made of pork!'

Maybe a few lines to show the best intent
Carefully imparting how is it meant:

START WITH
'Yes, I think that you're heaven sent!'
THEN (depending on your sex)
'And yes, you make me soaking wet!' OR
'And yes, you give me a trouser tent!'
THEN
'But when I see you, I'll shout out no more!'
'I won't hold up a card, giving you a score!'
'I'll act respectful and coy, all of the time'
'Won't hold a neon sign, saying 'Fancy a 69?''
'Respectfully yours'
'With a *Civil Phwoah!*'

It's Time

It's time!
Not to *tell the time*
But to *tell Time!*
'Please do stop!'
But, Time!
I realise I won't get a reply!
I know you're not a speaking clock!
I think about days that've gone by
And those days that I've still got
Time! You've got to stop!

Because if you don't, what awaits me?
A dodgy bladder? Crumbling knees?
Foggy brain, sagging skin and grey hair?
Dribbling, shouting and *the thousand yard stare*?
Then a hole in the ground to end my days?
Or in an urn as my final resting place?

So, Time, you're the fourth dimension!
And way above my comprehension!
An abstract concept, apparently!
Whatever *that* is, it's beyond me!

It's time!
To tell Time!
Where did you go?
Why did you travel so fast?
Where were you off to in such a hurry?
Were you very late for something?

Time, take your time - we don't mind waiting!
Please can you stop your date from updating!

Can you just take a pause?
There are too many scores on the birthday doors!
Can you please lessen the haste?
Perhaps a little less pace?
There are already too many candles on the cake!

It's time!
To tell Time!
Please, stop!
Sit down, take those trainers off!

If you won't stop, then crawl!
No need to be in a rush at all!
It is improbable, but I must ask...
Could you turn round and go back?

Praise for Sauce

Named Quotes:

"I always said he'd never amount to anything! Reading this proves my point!" - David's school headmaster.

"Abominable!" - A. Yeti

"Abdominal!" – P. Andre

"Covid, Brexit and now this!!!! Have we not suffered enough?!" – Geradine Bumblesplat

"Mein Kampf for the Google Generation" – A.H.

"Available in all bad bookshops and the libraries of mental institutions" – D. Ranged

Anonymous Quotes:

"A real page and stomach turner!"

"Best read *At Stool!*"

"I've always advocated that people should read but now, I'm not so sure!"

"How many trees died so this book could get made?"

"When I read this, just for a minute, I think the Nazis were right to burn books!"

"If those who had fought in the war had known that one of their own countrymen would go onto produce this, then they wouldn't have bothered!"

"David thinks a stanza is a Japanese car!"

"Once you get past the first 236 pages, it's fine!"

"I enjoyed a bit of this book and that was the bit that said 'The End'!"

"The worst thing committed to paper since my bottom!"

"Definitely a book for in the toilet. And I mean IN the toilet! It takes a few flushes to go down..."

"What is David like as a poet? Well, if Pam Ayers had been a docker..."

Printed in Dunstable, United Kingdom